Imogen Cunningham:

A PORTRAIT

Imogen Cunningham, self-portrait, about 1910

Imogen Cunningham:
A PORTRAIT

by Judy Dater

in association with The Imogen Cunningham Trust

NEW YORK GRAPHIC SOCIETY · BOSTON

First edition

All rights, title, and interest in the works of Imogen Cunningham are the property of The Imogen Cunningham Trust. Prints of her photographs may be purchased from the Trust at 1713 Grove Street, Berkeley, California 94709.

The publishers are grateful to Manroot, South San Francisco, California, for permission to reprint James Broughton's poem, "Everything Is Connected," which was first published in the collection of his work entitled *Odes for Odd Occasions*.

New York Graphic Society books are published by Little, Brown and Company. Published simultaneously in Canada by Little, Brown and Company (Canada) Limited.

LIBRARY OF CONGRESS CATALOGING IN PUBLICATION DATA

Main Entry under title:

Imogen Cunningham: a portrait.

1. Cunningham, Imogen, 1883–1976. 2. Photography, Artistic. 3. Photographers—United States—Biography. I. Cunningham, Imogen, 1883–1976. II. Dater, Judy. III. Imogen Cunningham Trust.
TR140.C78147   770'.92'4 [B]   79–2375
ISBN 0-8212-0751-2

PRINTED IN THE UNITED STATES OF AMERICA

Contents

Acknowledgments

Working on this book I have felt very close to Imogen; in providing its substance she has left me the greatest gift possible. It has brought me months of unexpected adventure, traveling from Maine to Hawaii, meeting many of her old friends and associates, making new friends myself. I am glad of this opportunity to express my thanks to all those who helped me in the exciting process of putting this book together.

The book could not have existed if I had not had the very special cooperation of The Imogen Cunningham Trust. The three trustees, Arthur Shartsis, Adrian Wilson, and Gryffyd Partridge, gallantly gave me free rein to do the book as I wished, and put the indispensable resources of the Trust at my disposal. They gave me access to all Imogen Cunningham's personal papers and correspondence, to interviews and other written material about her, and permitted me to search through all her files of negatives, proofs, and prints. But I could not have taken full advantage of this material without the marvelous organization of Danee McFarr, Administrator of The Imogen Cunningham Trust. My wish was her command. She knew immediately where to find anything I needed and often tipped me off to a bit of memorabilia she had discovered earlier. And Danee was great company in the office, sharing my excitement as I went through the letters and snapshots. She played an important role in making this book.

The Imogen Cunningham prints reproduced here were prepared by Rondal Partridge. He donated many hours and much energy to painstakingly printing and reprinting Imogen's original negatives to achieve the best possible results, and I am most grateful to him.

I am immeasurably indebted to Imogen's family and to her friends and associates for granting me interviews and permitting me to publish their reminiscences of her. Each interview turned out to be a memorable experience as Imogen broke the ice, and each person was more open and giving than I could have hoped. I regret that for a number of reasons, notably the lack of space, I could use only a small part of the splendid material they gave me.

A great many individuals—too many to list all of them separately, unfortunately—helped in different ways. I am grateful to all the photographers who generously lent their photographs of Imogen for reproduction in the book. I would also like to thank particularly Roi Partridge, for his support and candor; Padraic and Marjorie Partridge, for their great good humor; Edna Bullock, for her gracious permission to reprint her letter from Imogen; Andrea Turnage and S. W. Samore, for their important editorial contributions; and Katy Homans, for her beautiful book design. Betty Childs, senior editor of New York Graphic Society, deserves a special accolade for giving shape and substance to all this material. I cannot imagine working with an editor who could have grasped the intent of all this any better, and her sensitivity and enthusiasm made her a joy to work with.

Finally, I am deeply grateful to Tim Hill, formerly editor-in-chief of New York Graphic Society, for conceiving the idea for the book and for having faith in me to carry it out.

J. D.

INTRODUCTION

Imogen with Ansel Adams and Jerry Uelsmann (also known as "Jerry Uelsmann Receiving the Baptism of the GodPhotographers of the West"), Point Lobos, 1969 TED ORLAND

Introduction

I'm not so curious about everybody's life. I like biography myself, but I don't like little snips of questions and answers. I like somebody who really knows what he's writing about. Now the other day a man came to interview me about Dorothea Lange. That's the way to do it, wait until I'm dead and get the real truth from someone who knew me.[1]

—IMOGEN CUNNINGHAM

Imogen may have thought that getting the real truth about her would be a simple task, but after interviewing forty close friends, relatives, associates, photographers, writers, artists, and historians I still wonder what is her true story.

I met Imogen about fifteen years ago when I was a beginning photography student. She was participating in a symposium at Big Sur Hot Springs on the life and work of Edward Weston. Many of my photographic heroes were there— among them, Ansel Adams, Wynn Bullock, Cole and Brett Weston, Peter Stackpole, Jack Welpott. Imogen struck me immediately as a very special person. I wanted to talk to her or make some contact, even though I really didn't know much about her or her work. In fact, I knew very little about photography, but I was an eager young sponge. I can't remember who spoke first, but my guess is that she started the conversation. I was incredibly shy at the time, something Imogen was not, and I can almost hear her saying, "Come with me, I want to photograph you." She made a portrait of me at Big Sur, and afterward she invited me to her home, asked me to bring some prints, and was generally very friendly and open. I was overwhelmed and flattered, and after I returned to San Francisco I phoned her to set a time when I would come by. That was the beginning of a wonderful friendship.

I was always in awe of Imogen, inspired by her, amused, thrilled, delighted, and surprised. I think my total admiration of her, something she really sneered at, clouded my vision of her as a real person. While I loved and admired her, as so many other people did, I didn't know her completely; there was always an air of mystery surrounding her and her life, certain missing pieces to the puzzle. It has been a little over a year and a half since her death on June 24, 1976. I have spent the past ten months interviewing people who knew her, examining her work, reading her voluminous correspondence (she kept carbon copies of every letter she wrote, and there were thousands), and perusing every article I could find about her.

I know more about her now, feel closer than ever, and have even greater admiration for her accomplishments as an artist and as a human being. Though many of the pieces have fallen into place, there still remains some mystery and many contradictions surrounding her life. I believe that is the way she wanted it. Her statement, "Wait until I'm dead and get the real truth from someone who knew me," seems now like a challenge she threw down, daring anyone to pick it up, knowing it would be impossible, somehow enjoying her own private joke.

Imogen is difficult, if not impossible to sum up. Her life was a complex one, and I am left with strong impressions that have in part been confirmed by the people who speak in this book. She was certainly a courageous woman, one with a mind of her own, who worked hard all of her life. The fact that as a young woman she chose to go into photography and into chemistry as an avenue to photography, both fields that were traditional male preserves, apparently did not seem remarkable to her. There was no conscious feminism involved. If she was devoted to any cause, it was to work. In January 1913 she wrote an article about women in photography for *The Arrow*, her University of Washington sorority magazine. In it she said, "Being devoted to one's work is much like hearing a great Wagnerian opera with one's soul open. The energy and vitality of life seem for a time sapped but come back in renewed quantity and quality." Imogen was involved and productive all her life, until a week before she died at the age of ninety-three. Work sustained her, gave her life and energy, and made her much sought after by different types of people of all ages.

Her work and her involvement with people are what made Imogen tick. She was a great photographer who would often say, "I photograph anything that light falls on." But when you review her oeuvre, you see that people, both as nudes and as portraits, are her major theme. She said: "People began to interest me very early. I

don't know why. Perhaps . . . because in people there are no duplicates. You must say that. If you see a sunrise it happens another day, too, but people are always different, they are different every second."

Imogen thrived on her photographic métier and was surrounded by fascinating people, but she was also a wife and mother for a major part of her life. For her, this was an essential experience. She was married in 1915 to the etcher Roi Partridge. Their meeting and coming together is a tender and touching love story. Roi was living and working in Paris in 1913, while Imogen was in Seattle. Roi was also from Seattle and they had mutual friends, Clare Shepard and John Butler, but Roi and Imogen had never met. Imogen started corresponding with him because she

Imogen Cunningham, 1908 AKEYAMA

chaired the entertainment committee of the Fine Arts Society and arranged the society's afternoon teas, where she would sell his prints. When she was successful she would write and send him a check. Their correspondence quickly passed the business stage and a kind of courtship began. Roi was charmed by Imogen's honesty, pepperiness, and intelligence, which came through in her letters to him even then. Imogen was captivated by this very handsome artist, who wrote gloriously romantic letters to her on huge sheets of paper, 18 x 24 inches. From one of them:

I got out that Town Crier *article about you today and pinned it up. That certainly is a marvelous little fotograf. I sometimes wish, however, horrid man that I am, that the fotos I have of you were a little less artistic so that I might see a little more of you. The little snap-shot shows the most but is the least beautiful. No two of the three seem to be of the same person. My kingdom for more, Miss. I rule over wide domains. Very beautiful, with cities that outshine Samarkand and vales that outshine Cashmere. There are towers with tinkling bells on the corners and strange mustached men below in yellow silk with blue and cloth-of-gold. There the sun in summer will shine. In Paris in summer he does not shine. How can he shine in two places at once? Good night.*

In these letters he talks about the children they will have, their names, where they will go on vacations, and how wonderful their life will be together. Eventually he proposes marriage. How could she resist? After about a year of writing and exchanging photographs, Roi returned to the United States, forced to leave Europe because of the war. Shortly after arriving in Seattle he met Imogen, and within a few months they were married. Their first child, Gryffyd, was born within the year, and the twin boys, Rondal and Padraic, shortly after.

Circumstances had forced the family to move from Seattle to California, and they finally settled in Oakland. Roi taught art at Mills College, and Imogen raised her boys, never ceasing to photograph. She was restricted to the house for several years as a young mother, though she never spoke of it as confinement. She voiced her feelings about having children in a number of

letters. In July 1951 she wrote to her son Pad and daughter-in-law Marjorie:

I feel that no woman has really lived without the experience of motherhood and most men do not grow up without the responsibility of fatherhood. I can see the reasons for not wanting to bring a child into a world like ours, but the personal reasons for having children usually outweigh the philosophic ones for not having them. The young men of today are not being sealed off from fatherhood — they participate, and I have observed they are a lot more interested in their children than if they just looked at them once in a while and were not allowed to see the problems of having children. . . . I am not a silly sentimentalist over babies but if they are well, are handled rightly, they conform to living a good deal better than most grown-ups.

In a letter written to a woman in May 1973, she said: "It seems to me that children are the only reason for marriage but not to be made the only

Roi Partridge, about 1915 IMOGEN CUNNINGHAM

interest. Some women I know who could have been good artists make the children a reason for NOT working any more." Imogen certainly never allowed this to happen. Rather than neglect her creative interests she worked at home, photographing the boys and the items they would bring her—a snake, for instance—and many of her famous plant forms and flowers were done when the children were young.

Life with Roi and their three sons continued until 1934, with Imogen pursuing her photography all of this time. That year she was asked to come to New York for a few weeks on assignment for *Vanity Fair* magazine. The offer led to an important turning point in her life and career. She wanted very much to go. Her boys were independent teenagers, and she felt it was time for her to do something for herself. There had been friction at home with Roi, and her decision to make the trip, over his protest, was the catalyst that ended the marriage. Almost immediately after she returned from New York, Roi went to Reno for a divorce. She was on her own. This was to be her only marriage, and it is still a mystery why she never remarried or apparently never had a close physical relationship with any other man.

Imogen stayed on in her house in Oakland; she continued working for *Vanity Fair* and she made portraits for a living. She was also a member of the influential photographic circle called Group f/64. This was a small group of photographers— including Ansel Adams, Willard Van Dyke, and Edward Weston—who held similar views on photography. They had abandoned soft focus romanticism and were seeking absolute sharpness and clarity in their images. Imogen always described the group as little more than an excuse for these friends to get together and socialize. They did have one important group show in San Francisco in 1932. She talked a little bit about this group in an interview with Margery Mann:

I can't remember that it lasted longer than the first exhibition we gave at the de Young Museum. I made a proposition at that time that every one of us, regardless of what we were interested in, photograph each other and make a show. But it came to nothing. I guess I didn't speak loud enough. You know, as a matter of fact, I had no confidence in myself, and I didn't have anybody that helped me to have it. I was just being constantly knocked down. The stuff that I did in the thirties—no one paid any attention to it except that I'd sell it at the Mills College shop that was on the campus. Every once in a while I'd sell something.

This period must have been particularly hard for her, both emotionally and financially, but her inner strength and determination pulled her through and kept her going. Her fame as a portrait photographer grew, but she always had to work very hard to make even a meager living. She lived simply; even after the considerable financial success that came very late in life she remained quite frugal.

Photography was her life. After moving to San Francisco in 1947 and establishing herself in her little white frame cottage on Green Street, she taught for a time at the San Francisco Institute of Fine Arts (now the San Francisco Art Institute), and she was often a guest lecturer at the art schools and museums in the Bay Area. She had strong opinions about photography and made them known. Imogen had a reputation for being sharp-tongued and acidic, but in her photography a strong romanticism often came through. I found evidence of this in her notes for an address given at the Oakland Museum in March 1965. (Her penchant for never throwing anything out provided me with notes for various talks she gave in the sixties) On 3 x 5 cards she had written: "The formula for doing a good job in photography: Is to think like a poet. There are many choices, but at the moment, I recommend Tagore, who wrote: 'My soul is alight with your infinitude of stars. Your world has broken upon me like a flood. The flowers of your garden blossom in my body. The joy of life that is everywhere burns like an incense in my heart. And the breath of all things plays on my life as on a pipe of reeds.'" This lyrical, gentle poem is, I believe, a key to understanding Imogen's deepest sensibilities, as expressed not only in her work but in her life.

More detailed observations about photography were made in notes for a lecture at San Francisco State University in December 1963:

I will not try to tell you how to make a successful portrait—to be honest, I really do not know. I can only offer a few ideas of personal necessity, and the first is empathy—that is a common word today, but it was coined by Tichner when I was a student of psychology and at the time was understood as a translation of the German Sich in etwas einfühlen. For me this is as good a definition of the word now as it was more than fifty years ago. It has nothing to do with the aesthetic feeling on seeing a thing or a person. It also does not mean sympathy with a person. Feeling ourselves into and learning to know another is not easy—in fact it is almost unattainable. So in the end the photographer has to be satisfied with a contemplation of the shape. Even this is not a small assignment. If one can succeed in getting some kind of an aesthetic result out of it—so much the better. From now on it is largely an intuitive process which can be best perfected by time and experience. By that I mean practice combined with the use of an unknown such as illusive invention. There are no formulae and each person must feel his way into interpretation. The struggle between the idea and the image goes on.

When people talk about Imogen there are certain things that are mentioned over and over: her garden and love of plants, her attire, and her cooking. She felt as strongly about these as she did about photography. When I first moved from a small apartment in San Francisco to a house in Marin County with a very overgrown and neglected garden, she came to visit me and immediately told me everything that should be done—

Judy Dater, 1974 IMOGEN CUNNINGHAM

THE INTERVIEWS

Padraic and Marjorie Partridge JUDY DATER

CHAPTER I

The Family & the Mills College Years

PADRAIC AND MARJORIE PARTRIDGE

Padraic Partridge, mining engineer and geologist, one of Imogen's twin sons, and his wife, Marjorie

Pad: It was very interesting having Imogen as a mother. She could answer any question—not highly scientific ones, but questions about animals and plants and chemistry, and so on. Her photography didn't interfere with family living anywhere near as much as people have written. It wasn't all-time consuming. People came for sittings, and the rest—the darkroom—she did in her leftover time, after dinner or in the morning. So it didn't interfere. Remember—Imogen never drove a car. She didn't shop. She didn't go to the grocery store. She picked up the phone and it came in a box, or sometimes we picked things up. The boys kept house. They swept, scrubbed the floor, did the dishes. So when you simplify your life—not buying shoes for kids, not taking them to school or music classes—you have time to photograph. It's the only way to live if you are going to be a professional.

Imogen was the center of the home. Roi ruled as a stern disciplinarian. He didn't involve himself with the children—not with feeding or clothing us, or setting up a pigeon pen or a rat hutch, or anything. So without Imogen there would have been no organized family life.

That tells you something about Imogen and Roi. They were both highly professional people, and the house was structured for them. The matting or printing room was in the attic, and both the etchings and the photographs were cut and mounted there. The etching room and the darkroom were in the basement, and between the basement and main floor was a trapdoor. There was only one phone in the house and it was ringing constantly, and when it rang the trapdoor would go WHAM WHAM BAM against the wall, someone would holler, "Trap's open!" and rush to the phone. If you walked out of the kitchen or in the back door without looking, down the trap you went, twelve feet to the basement floor without hitting anything but some sharp stairs. Several people did that.

There were arguments in the family. Between Imogen and the kids, mostly. "Okay, you sloppy bums, clean up the kitchen." "Okay, if you're going to have supper, you're going to have to do the dishes. You can't live around here with a sink full of dishes." And there were arguments between Imogen and Roi. But they were fairly careful parents that way—they didn't quarrel too much in public. But sometimes after we went to bed we would hear arguments. Roi was an only child and he was raised to have what he wanted, the way he wanted it, and he demanded a certain order in things. I think that was one of the problems. He wanted more services, more housecleaning—he wanted a housewife in a sense, and he wasn't getting one. Imogen did her photography in her spare moments, and he assumed those spare moments were coming from him—and they probably were. At the same time he got a fantastic amount of service from Imogen as a hostess. Since he was a professor, he brought home a lot of people, all kinds: Navajo Indians visiting the west coast, artists, a great many students from Mills. He'd invite his friends over any time and they could stay for a month, and they often did. But he didn't like Imogen's friends to stay that long. We had the room. There was a chicken coop we made into a little house, and a double garage with a big room above it, and another small house—we rented that out, but sometimes it was available—so we could always put people up.

Another thing. Roi was very much concerned about economizing. It was a sort of Depression attitude, a fear of not having enough. There was constant pressure not to waste money. "Close the door, we can't afford heat going out!" "Don't wash your hands with the water running!" This in a place where water was ten cents a thousand gallons, something like that. So you turned on the faucet to wet your hands, turned it off, soaped up, turned the faucet back on to rinse them. This when Imogen was in the basement washing films with water running for an hour and a half. Imogen just couldn't think about things like that.

So Roi's attitude and Imogen's activities were not conducive to living smoothly together. But they were always very, very friendly until the day she died. He admired her work, though it was hard for him to think that he couldn't do as well in photography. But he does beautiful etching—absolutely out of this world. I really think there is no better etcher in the world.

Marjorie: They were both very professional artists. They both worked very hard, with an attitude toward art that you should have a life work and leave something for posterity—it's a nineteenth-century attitude. But both Imogen and Roi had it, and I think that's one of the reasons that when their careers conflicted they remained friends.

Pad: Both of them had that attitude early, and they even had the guts to express it—that they were working to put something away for posterity—not for their kids, but for the world. It's a form of conceit, and it's necessary for happiness in life.

I don't know whether you could say our childhood was normal. But what is normal? Edward Weston's kids would run through the house, grab a head of cabbage, slam it on the floor to break it open, and run off—talking with their mouths full, spewing bits of cabbage, donuts in one hand, bananas stuck under their belts, if they were wearing anything at all. And I thought that was normal, and maybe it was. Normal, according to me, is whatever people do. So I'd consider our childhood normal, but I do recognize that it was different. In our house we ate at the table most of the time, and most of the time the food was cooked, and most of the time served very nicely. We could have our friends over, and we could play whatever games we wanted. Imogen hardly ever criticized—her strongest criticism was one of silence. Imogen was a pretty good mother. She didn't interfere with us growing up.

Gryff and the twins

Every summer Roi went somewhere in the mountains to do his etching. Somewhere in Arizona or New Mexico. It was Roi's vacation, and the kids' vacation, but I don't know whether Imogen considered it vacation. Up to 1931 we had an open touring car, with a top but no sides. Everything fitted inside the bumpers and running boards—no trailers, no junk hanging out, no gasoline stoves, no tents. We had a tarp or a lean-to that tied to the car so the kids could sleep there if it rained, and the front seat of the car lay down to make a bed. Imogen did the cooking, on a grill sitting on rocks laid over a hole in the ground.

We went everywhere: the Canadian Rockies, New Mexico, the Sierra Nevada, Oregon, Washington, British Columbia. Roi was an excellent camper. He could spot a place to camp, he knew where the water was and whether it could be drunk. We'd just drive off the road and invariably we'd come to a very nice place. Often other people had camped there, and the kids—we didn't like it—picked up all the cans and trash, pulled all the nails out of the trees, took all the ropes down, dug a hole and buried it all. And left a very neat sign on a tree: "This campground was cleaned up by Roi Partridge and sons. Please leave it as you find it."

I didn't know people took mattresses with them camping until I was over sixteen. I thought people *liked* to sleep on the ground.

We were all still living together when Imogen went to New York. I don't remember when she left, or how, or how long she was gone. It wasn't a big deal for us. We were sixteen or seventeen—we could cook, we could wash dishes. It was a big deal for Roi, but not for the kids.

The divorce didn't seem to make any great change in Imogen's life. She just went right on—it was no traumatic thing.

Marjorie: Imogen and Roi had the most amiable relationship of any divorced people I've ever known. They went to the same parties, they liked the same people, they visited each other's houses, they kept track of each other. Roi saved many of her clippings. He once gave me a set of clippings and scrapbooks, publicity received when they were living together. Actually they were a very congenial couple, but they found it more comfortable to live with people who didn't make such demands on their time.

Pad: I don't know the financial arrangements of the divorce, but apparently Imogen got the house and some money, which was probably not enough. So she increased the amount of photography she did—very much. Later the boys scattered. Ron went into the Navy, Gryff went into the Navy, and even before that I went to the University of California and then transferred to the University of Nevada. The house was sold in 1944, I think, but I wasn't around. I never went back. The only thing that bothers me is that I had a box of dynamite hidden up in the attic, pretty well stashed away. I often wonder what will happen if that house burns down.

After the divorce she had to think about money —money to live on, to pay the taxes on the house—and I was in college, and every once in a while, though I never asked for it, she'd give me fifteen or twenty dollars. Of course, I didn't notice the lack of money. When you're raised in a

The twins, about 1924

house where the lights are being turned off all the time, you aren't given money. I don't remember my father giving me one single five-cent piece. Not a dime, nothing. But I did have ways to earn money. I was paid five cents for a mouse, ten cents for a rat, and I kept the neighborhood pretty well decimated. In fact I raised rats so I could let them go in the garden and catch them and get my ten cents. I did. How are you going to get fifty cents unless you get five big, fat black rats?

When I went to college I took chemistry. I didn't attempt to be an artist except in very minor ways. Ron and I both photographed, and I did a bit of art work at school that my teachers praised —but not my family. Their standards were far too high. Roi never praised anyone who attempted to make an etching with less than fifty years experience. Maybe a hundred. And Imogen was the same.

So I took chemistry at first. Mostly because I wanted to know more of what Imogen was talking about. She had taken chemistry at the University of Washington and later took an advanced degree in Germany, and I was pretty impressed with what she knew. But I found that chemistry at the University of California in the thirties, after the first two years, was really a course in atomic particles. I could understand it, but not mathematically. And I didn't enjoy calculating 6.3542 billion electron volts, for instance. So I lost interest, and I consulted Imogen about what I should do. She asked me what I was working at in the summer, and I told her I was working in a mine, I was a miner. She said, "Don't you want to know more about rocks?" So I changed to the mining department on her suggestion. She influenced me, but in a very simple way. She never tried to read you, or to pin you down.

Marjorie: Imogen had a very good analytical mind, and I respected her opinion a great deal. She'd just talk to you and her intuitive analysis of a situation would point you in the right direction.

Pad: When Roi was at Mills, she invited all the students, and they came, as many as thirty at a time. Sometimes I was ushered out of the room because private conversations were going on about how to live, love, and learn. The girls were using Imogen as a kind of guide for living.

Marjorie: A great many of the students at Mills needed to talk to somebody, and Imogen was one of the most straight-thinking people on sex I have ever known. She didn't have a Victorian attitude.

Pad: I don't know about any boyfriends of Imogen's. She was always going out—to all kinds of exhibits, all kinds of museums, all kinds of musical things. She didn't drive, and lots of people took her places. When she was ninety, twenty-year-old fellows would take her to concerts, and so would old wobble Charlie, also ninety. But I can't remember any boyfriends except one. He was a banker, had a big black Chrysler with horns on the fenders. A million dollars had disappeared from his bank, but he said he would put up no defense because his very loyal employees had made an error, and it was as much his fault as theirs because he hadn't watched them closely. So he went gaily off to prison for four or five years, and when he came out he dug it up. He was a great guy—had imagination. He was the only boyfriend I know of. I assume that she was not very much oriented toward relationships involving sexuality. Attraction, flirting, they just didn't seem to involve her. If she did have boyfriends, she was the most discreet mother I've ever seen.

Somewhere along the line she got an image of herself. I don't remember how or when it started, but I remember her saying a few amazing things. Once, just after the war, I said to her, "How come you never married again? I mean, you were young, you were good looking, you were an artist and you had a lot of men around. There was that banker with the big Chrysler. Maybe you didn't know it, but every time he came he used to bring us a quart of whiskey and tell us to bug off. There were a lot of guys, and that one had a million bucks. How come you didn't marry him?" "Well," she said, "he was older than I, and I didn't want to be nursemaid to some old fart." And I said, "Yes, but you were young and vital, how about sex and all that interesting stuff?" She said, "Well, I'm not dead yet." She was over sixty then. That was about the time I noticed she was saying things for effect rather than giving straight answers.

About that time she started wearing a cape rather than a coat. But the image didn't really develop until she was teaching, with the students sitting at her feet in reverence to her majestic thoughts. Her teaching was largely a compilation of smart cracks, but most of them were right on.

Marjorie: She started wearing the peace symbol right after Hiroshima. It became a hippie symbol later, but she wore it since the war. To her it meant Ban the Bomb.

Pad: She didn't like the bomb. She never said anything to me about it—I was highly involved in mining uranium for the first atomic bomb—but she was against it.

Marjorie: When Imogen came to visit us she'd often spend the afternoon writing letters. A great many of her correspondents were people she had known for a lifetime. Most of us seem to lose track of people, but Imogen kept her friends all through her life. That's unusual.

Pad: She kept friends from college, and many from the days in Germany. When we cleaned out her things we found an incredible amount of stuff—for instance, she kept the names and addresses of everyone at her table on the boat she went to Germany on in 1909, and later she wrote to them. And she kept up with Roi's old friends. She spent hours and hours at the typewriter, right up to the last hour. Many times she'd hand me a bundle of ten, twelve letters—every day, ten, twelve letters. And when she went back to Germany in 1960 she looked up people she'd known in 1909. Fifty years—a hell of a time to keep friends.

ROI PARTRIDGE

Roi Partridge, etcher, Imogen's former husband

In 1911 I took a studio in Paris. I was about twenty-three or -four, and I'd been traveling around Germany and Italy with another art student from Seattle, having a wonderful time, and I decided to settle in Paris for a while. Back in Seattle I had worked with a chap named John Butler and a girl named Clare Shepard—we called ourselves The Triad—and after I'd been working in Paris a while these friends arranged an exhibition of my work and sold things. They sent me a large check—three thousand francs—that I lived on for a long time. Imogen was a friend of theirs, though I'd never met her, and she had something to do with it. She wrote me about the exhibition and we corresponded back and forth and she sent me a beautiful photograph—she was a charming girl. I stayed in Paris earning enough as a printmaker to live, corre-

sponding with Imogen all this time. Then the war came and I returned to Seattle late in 1914, and within a few months we were married. And nine months later we had our first child. Imogen was working as a photographer and earning money, and I was selling a few prints, so between the two of us we had enough to live on.

We lived in a tiny studio. A little cottage with a fireplace standing alone in the middle of the room. We had all sorts of experiences then. Rabindranath Tagore, the Indian writer, came there once. He was the most dignified and handsome man I ever saw. I don't think Imogen photographed him, though. She was busy with her photography, so we had a very nice Swedish girl to help us take care of the child. One night an uncle of mine took us to the theater, and while we were out the house caught on fire. The girl had grabbed the child and run out and set off the fire alarm, and the fire department came and put it out, but there was much excitement. I wrote my uncle about it, and he wrote back, "Get rid of that girl—she's a pyromaniac!" But we thought, my goodness, he can't know that after seeing the girl for less than half an hour. So we kept her on. Then Imogen was pregnant again. She was apt to be upset when she was pregnant, so we decided it would be better if I went away for a time. I was on a sketching trip to Carmel, intending to stay for a month or so, when I got word that the house had been set on fire again. I telegraphed asking whether I should return, but Imogen wired me to stay put. And

then a third fire occurred, and Imogen announced that she was coming down to Carmel. So she did, and she left my plates behind in the basement and I never saw them again. Shortly after that the twins, Rondal and Padraic, were born.

There I was in San Francisco—rather tragically, without means of earning a good living. In Seattle I had made some money out of prints, but now I had to get a job quickly. I found one as a poster designer with an advertising firm named Foster and Kleiser—the artist Maynard Dixon was working there too—and at the same time I got work teaching at a fashionable girls' school. Part of my job at the advertising firm was to take photographs of the billboards de-

Roi Partridge JUDY DATER

signed by the firm, and I'd take the negatives into Marcia's Photographers' Shop in lower San Francisco and have them developed. The girl who worked there had personality and charm and would talk about the prints. "That last lot was unusually good . . ." and so on. She turned out to be Dorothea Lange.

Dorothea married Maynard Dixon. I remember that Maynard and Imogen and I went for some dancing lessons with her. Dorothea had had polio and walked with a limp that she was anxious to overcome. So we went dancing, and dancing did help her limp. It was hard to notice in later years.

Then I was teaching at Mills, and we met a great many people, and life was very full. We had a normal family life, I suppose. The boys are typical. [*Interjection by May Ellen, Roi's wife: "They are* not *typical, not typical at all."*] I mean they carried through life certain characteristics they had as children. Gryffyd was the careful one who always hung his clothes neatly over the chair at night—that sort of thing—whereas the twins would undress and throw everything into the corners. Their room was full of old parts of radios and frogs and snakes and old machinery and I don't know what, but that was their character, and it's okay. They are so different from Gryffyd; he's so very careful and dignified, and they are still happy-go-lucky, adventurous, particularly Ron.

Most people use family names, but we wanted names that weren't so commonplace. The eldest was Gryffydd—though he doesn't spell it that way anymore—and Padraic was named after the Irish poet Padraic Colum, and Rondal—I don't know, just because of Ronald, it was Rondal. Gryffyd got his degree in architecture, Rondal has ably pursued a photographic career, and Padraic studied mining engineering and geology for six years. He knows his stuff very well. He's been sent to Bali and Java, and he's specialized in clays and industrial minerals.

We all used to go on camping trips. I remember once we went to Santo Domingo, the Indian reservation in New Mexico, to see a ceremonial dance. The boys were about eight or nine, and ordinarily children that age would lose interest very quickly and make a lot of trouble, but the

Imogen, Clare Shepard,
John Butler, about 1913

boys were so interested in this Indian dance that they stayed from nine in the morning to seven-thirty at night without the least bit of fuss. They were as fascinated as we were. You felt these Indians were serious—they were dancing for rain, first the summer kiva, then the winter kiva, going back and forth, dancing all day long. We met some of the Indians out here in California. John Collier, who was interested in the Indians and their welfare, had brought some of them out to the coast. One night we rode around the public square in Sante Fe and an Indian put up his hand and stopped us. It was one of the men we'd met in California, Tony Luhan. He said, "You were in Santa Fe and you never came to see us!" —as if it were a tragedy. A very nice chap. He'd

married an American writer, Mabel Dodge, and later on she wanted to divorce him, but people said the government wouldn't let her—she'd married him and she was going to stay with him.

We made other trips of that sort: Acoma Pueblo, and the Sierras, and Canada. And all the time I was etching and etching, wherever we went.

Ultimately our marriage broke up. I won't go into those details, but in the course of time it did, and I married a charming girl named Marion Lyman. She lived only five years—her death nearly bowled me over. But then I met the very delightful woman who is now my wife, and we've been happy ever since. I was married to Imogen for nineteen years, and I've been married to May Ellen for thirty-seven years, and they have been

Roi Partridge and his sons, about 1919

the most happy and serene years of my life.

Imogen's artistic interests were entirely given to photography, and she was quite excellent. Back in Seattle, before I knew her, she got a job working for the noted photographer of Indians—actually, he wasn't very much noted then—Edward S. Curtis. He spent his time traveling among the Indians, taking innumerable small photographs. Curtis wasn't an artist, but he had a German technician running his laboratory in Seattle who *was* an artist. He took those snapshots and cropped them and enlarged them and worked with them and made them into some of the finest photographs that had ever been made of the American Indian. Imogen got the job when she started at the University of Washington. She was working three days a week at Curtis's studio, I think, and she still got her degree in three years instead of four. Imogen's job was making the original prints for the portfolios of large gravures that accompanied each of the published volumes of Curtis's Indian photographs. I understand they were platinum prints, so she had to learn to print in this difficult medium.

One of my first appearances in Seattle newspaper columns was because of a photograph Imogen had taken of me in the mountains, running around without any clothes on. Some newspaperman got hold of it, and it made an interesting little item. I had been up at Mount Rainier sketching, and Imogen came up to visit me. She was photographing wherever she was, so she suggested I take my clothes off and pose for her. So there I was, sitting on a cake of ice and getting photographed in the buff. Luckily she was using soft focus lenses in those days, so the identification wasn't very exact.

She made you work hard. She would tell you what she wanted you to do, and she always had a point of view. She was always a sharp-tongued person with a point of view.

She made some very good photographs. I like the earlier ones more than the later ones perhaps, but she seems to be having amazing success, and I wouldn't interfere with that. I hope she continues to have it. The success she had in her later life led to some interesting things. I remember the picnic we attended in Golden Gate Park for her ninetieth birthday. And then after she died there was another celebration in her honor in Golden Gate Park in a wide, sunny meadow. So many of her friends were there, and her relatives, and old Mills students, and a lot of characters. The place was full of people with cameras, so that any time the boys and I were together we were surrounded by people click-clicking away. And there were some dancers—perhaps Imogen had photographed them, and so they had been asked to entertain. Five, six belly dancers, if you please, and they were beautiful. I have some very fine photographs of that occasion, of those dancers, and the table spread with bread and cheese and wine and fancy cakes. It was a really notable occasion. When you stop to think of it, how many people do you know whose death would be celebrated by a picnic in Golden Gate Park? Not the usual religious ceremony, but a lot of people gathering together who knew Imogen, who were fond of her and had admired her work. I think it was just the right way to celebrate the occasion: not with sadness but with happiness, and in a lovely setting in Golden Gate Park. The belly dancers, yes. . . .

ROGER STURTEVANT
Roger Sturtevant, photographer

I first met Roi and Imogen at a party at Dorothea Lange's—quite a party! Edward Weston was in town for the first time, and I believe he was the guest of honor. At any rate, there was Edward, and Anne Brigman, Imogen and Roi, Johan Hagemeyer, I think, and Dorothea, and Maynard

Dixon. Someone took one of those silly gag photographs, where Edward Weston and Anne Brigman posed as the mother and father of photography, cradling in their arms Dorothea's studio camera draped with a focusing cloth, and then grouped down below were the bastard children. It was a very silly picture, one that I would give my eyeteeth to have right now.

I saw a great deal of Roi and Imogen when Roi was working at Mills College. I was in and out of their fantastic household, which was livelier than the one in *You Can't Take It With You!* Weekends were for entertainment, Sunday usually. Roi would be down in the basement running proof prints or etching; Imogen would be washing prints in the darkroom; someone would be popping up and down the trapdoor of the kitchen;

the twins and Gryff and a few of their friends would be running in and out—and somehow or other Imogen would serve a very delicious dinner to God knows how many people. I still try to do spinach the way she did. There was a long kind of refectory table, and people from Mills College would be there, and Anne Brigman was there frequently. It was terribly informal.

The twins were fantastic. They would come up to you, these little redheaded boys, talking at absolutely breakneck speed. One would start a sentence and talk until he was out of breath, and then the other one would take over—exactly in the middle of a word. They were completely interchangeable, so you would never know who started a sentence and who finished it. And then, of course, at the same time, Roi and Imogen were

Roger Sturtevant, about 1922
IMOGEN CUNNINGHAM

doing all of their things, and rushing out to the garden and watering this and planting that, back and forth—it was quite a household.

It was about that time that Imogen did the beautiful photograph of the magnolia blossom. Other people had done it before, and I don't know how many thousands have done it since, but Imogen made the beautiful one. And about then Imogen did some photographs of me. At that time I affected bohemian clothes, but I wasn't dressing in a uniform the way hippies do now, all in jeans, and so on. I had one thing I liked very much, a Chinese coolie coat, and I wore sandals—nobody wore sandals except in Paris, but I didn't know that. So Imogen photographed me in the coolie coat sitting in a wicker chair underneath this big Japanese lantern they had in their living room, and there was the big refectory table in the middle of the room where everyone ate. She also did some photographs of me that were some of the most luscious pictures of a youth you have ever seen.

The years went by and Roi and Imogen got divorced. We saw each other every once in a while, and we never lost the original natural, almost familial feeling, right up to her death. During World War II I got a job from some construction company to go up to Seattle and photograph, but I didn't want to go because I was being

father, mother, wage earner, and everything else to my fifteen-year-old son. He had left his mother and come to live with me in San Francisco in the studio on Montgomery Street, and I didn't want to leave him alone there. So Imogen volunteered to come and baby-sit. She moved in. It was like *The Man Who Came to Dinner*. After I came back she didn't live there, but she kept on working in the studio and spending all of her days there for a year and a half. Finally it got so crowded that I said, "Imogen, you've just got to find a darkroom of your own." She was quite gregarious; she preferred living and working with someone.

Imogen was very funny. She was always coming up with funny things in this acid little manner. When Roi was in his heyday at Mills, and Imogen had become quite well known too, they were invited to a large dinner party by this woman who had decided to be a lion hunter, and the lions had to be in the arts. So at the party the hostess went around in a circle to introduce the celebrities—"my guests, the artists and writers." Each one said what he did. One was a writer, one was an artist, and when she came to Roi, Roi was a teacher and etcher. But when she came to Mrs. Partridge, Imogen said, "I do animal husbandry"—which was absolutely apt at the time, with those wild kids.

RONDAL PARTRIDGE, *part 1*
Rondal Partridge, photographer, one of Imogen's twin sons

Basically, Imogen was an early hippie. That came from her father. His name was, I think, Isaac Burns Cunningham, and I almost got called Isaac Burns Partridge and my twin brother Archibald Ebenezer Partridge. Imogen's father grew up on what his family called a plantation in Kentucky, with maybe four slaves, and they were rather poor. He got a very catch-as-catch-can education from visiting "professors" who gave exercises in logic or algebra or rhetoric in store-

fronts, and then when he was about twelve or thirteen he ran away to join the Union Army. My grandfather was a mystic, a seeker after the real truth, and he studied every religion he could find. When Imogen was fifteen or so her father took her to a religious commune in Port Angeles, Washington, where they cut down trees, and prayed, and practiced vegetarianism. Her father was of a gentle nature. He never drank or swore, and he was so horrified if he saw a horse being beaten that he'd buy the horse—so naturally he ended up pretty poor. In Seattle he had a contract for leveling the streets, and before that he was a grocery clerk in Portland. He used to teach me great tricks for tying knots in a hurry, or breaking string.

That experience of vegetarianism at the commune affected Imogen all her life. She was into every food fad—tiger's milk, wheat germ—and milk. She thrust quarts and quarts of milk on her children. I remember when I was about thirteen or fourteen in summer camp, I got up one morning and urinated white. I went roaring off to the camp doctor. It was sort of embarrassing at that age, and the doctor happened to be a woman—but it was just milk, a surplus of calcium. Anyway, Imogen's faddism caused her to feed us with a diet superior to the neighborhood diet, which was really pretty bad.

Of course our diet wasn't completely healthy. Imogen had a terrible sweet tooth, and I can't remember a single day, not one day, when I lived with my mother that there wasn't a cake or homemade candy in the house. And that came from her father too. He was fanatically opposed to organized religion, and he used to keep his children away from church on Sunday by organizing big candy bakeoffs every Sunday.

There was no religion in our family, and I think that too was a result of my grandfather's background. I believe he came from an Irish family that immigrated to Jamestown as indentured servants. Anyway, he inculcated an anti-Catholic position in his children. Imogen used to hum a little doggerel song to herself: "Kill a papist every day . . ." Honest, a little Irish jig. She never made racial jokes, but she did make a few jokes about Catholics—she was always talking about Catholics. It was strange growing up with the combination of her prejudices and my father's, and bringing myself up in the opposite way.

Her father's attitudes influenced Imogen, but sometimes in a negative way. Her stance that she was liberated and that she could do whatever she wanted was mostly a reaction to the way her father treated her mother: friendly and pleasant, but as if she were a child-slave. He never shouted at her, he never rode her, but he expected her to

get up at five and work until seven at night, and I suppose perform the wifely duties thereafter. Imogen's sister Paula always claimed that their mother didn't know how to read or write, though Imogen denied it. In any case her mother was, in a way, a tremendous influence. Imogen was set in her mind that that wasn't what the female role should be. She always said, "I don't have to join the lib party. I *am* liberated." She was in sympathy with the suffragists in the twenties, and of course she favored all other liberal causes. She voted for Eugene Debs in 1920, and she voted Socialist every time Norman Thomas ran for president. I don't think she even defected for Roosevelt.

My father and mother never got along a day in their lives. They loved each other very much, but they never got along. Roi was absolutely dogmatic and sometimes crabby, so Imogen would invite people to dinner, because at least he couldn't be crabby with people there. He'd become pleasant then. Imogen was very gregarious anyway, and intelligent, good company, so all the visiting artists and art historians and professors, people like that, would come by, and there was never a week without a dozen or maybe twenty people coming to dinner.

Both my parents underestimated their twins. Perhaps it was something about our being twins, having a special relationship to each other different from anything else in this world that they couldn't understand. Pad and I were sort of hyperactive, full of joy of life. We used up everything around us—wore out shoes in six weeks, put holes through our pants. We dug forts and built tree houses, reinforcing each other. We were never bored.

Imogen was perceptive enough to see that with the way my father and I pushed heads the best thing was to ship me out, and I lived with relatives a lot. Then the day I finished high school I took off, and that was the end. I had forty-two cents and a 35-mm. camera and a developing tank. I followed the rodeo for a year—stood out in the middle of the rodeo field and photographed the riders, sold prints for one dollar each and came home after a year with four hundred dollars. Of course Roi thought it was a waste of time photographing cowboys. In fact it was an extraordinarily valuable experience, because I can stand in any dangerous, fast-moving situation —in the middle of a road, on top of a motor boat, in a herd of cattle—and think clearly enough to photograph and not get hurt. I've done countless dangerous things as a photographer. I've climbed power poles and been eighteen inches away from 20,000 volts, and I've walked eight-inch beams fifteen stories up, but you're just as safe there as anywhere if you can remember where you are. And I bloody well had to remember in the middle of a rodeo.

Imogen influenced me in the sense that she gave me leeway to do the crazy things I wanted to do. As it's turned out, people think I'm erratic, a character, but in a way I'm less of a character than anyone in the family. I mean I have to be the most responsible, the most reliable, to follow the discipline of photography. My God, you have to do every step right, one after the other, or it doesn't come out right. That's responsibility.

Rondal Partridge
JUDY DATER

GRYFFYD AND JANET PARTRIDGE

Gryffyd Partridge, architect, Imogen's oldest son, and his wife, Janet

Gryff: There was nothing that Imogen wasn't interested in, with the possible exception of automobiles and sports. She was interested in everything she was doing, everything we were doing, and in the world at large, so we had a very lively time.

I guess we took her energy for granted. She was always that way. When we were in school she was photographing plant forms and doing portraits. The people mostly came to the house because she couldn't drive. She never did learn, though I believe she was beginning to when our house caught fire. The damage wasn't severe, but I understand it was so traumatic for her that she never resumed the driving. Later on she justified not driving on the grounds that she would have been a chauffeur for the family. She didn't seem to miss it. During the war she would get out on the road and hitchhike, but we tried to discourage that.

She didn't try to influence me to be a photographer, though she did encourage me as soon as

Gryffyd Partridge JUDY DATER

I indicated an interest in architecture. From then on her gift to me would invariably be an architecture book. One thing she did inculcate in us was independence of thought—not to care what other people thought if we knew we were doing the right thing. She exemplified that in her own life. And one of her most telling influences on us is the fact that she didn't settle down when she turned sixty but stayed active until she was over ninety—a pretty good example for us all. She was absolutely unrelenting in the demands she made on herself as well as on others to accomplish what she intended, right up until the day she died.

Imogen rarely read anything other than biographies or art books, rarely novels. And she didn't read any political journals, didn't subscribe to *The Nation* or *The New Republic*, although for years she voted for Norman Thomas. My father's favorite reading was that notable Republican journal, *The Saturday Evening Post.* He was very conservative, and Imogen felt she cancelled him out politically.

I don't recall that they argued about politics, or that they argued a great deal about other things either. There was the one argument that precipitated their divorce, of course. Imogen had been asked to go to New York to meet the editor of *Vanity Fair* and do some photography, but my father wanted her at least to defer the trip until he could go with her. But she went anyway—that was in the early spring of 1934. In June, Roi went to Reno to get the divorce.

I never heard her speak of remarrying. She liked her freedom.

Imogen enjoyed her fame when it came. But she was a bit scornful of people who suddenly came to her to be photographed once she was famous. She said, in effect, "Why didn't they come years ago? I was just as good." Finally, in the last five years of her life she was making a good living, but not until then.

For one thing, she charged very little. And perhaps her style didn't attract as many sitters as it might have. Time and again she'd say that people weren't willing to be shown as they were, but she wanted to capture them—she used the term "nail"—with sharp photographs showing every pore. Still, she was not above making some slightly flattering photographs. That picture of Mrs. Wurlitzer comes to mind: a white-haired old lady against a black velvet backdrop. It's a good portrait, but I'm sure it's a bit flattering.

And she was not above arranging plant forms in special ways for her photographs; she was very interested in the decorative quality of plant forms. That *Aloe plicatilis*, for instance—she always used the Latin names of plants whenever she could—she used it in conjunction with hands and arranged it in a very decorative way.

Music was very important to Imogen too. One of her early friends, in the twenties, was Henry Cowell, the avant-garde composer. I don't think she read music, but she subscribed to *Modern Music*, a journal with scores by people like Cowell and Charles Ives. I've gone with her to concerts in which John Cage was beating out a non-tune on an old suitcase, or Henry Cowell was playing—with surprising melody—what he called tone clusters, hitting the piano keyboard with his forearm. And she really enjoyed it.

Imogen and Gryff, about 1917 (probably a self-portrait)

Janet: It was very interesting being her daughter-in-law, because you didn't feel daughter-in-lawzy. I remember her saying once, "I don't act like a mother-in-law, do I?" She was very conscious, trying not to interfere or criticize.

You felt she was a friend. And she was always ready to go somewhere to see something new. I'd call her up and she'd be perky and receptive, and she also had a tremendous background knowledge of whatever was involved—music, dance, a lecture—she wasn't going out of idle curiosity. I remember taking her to one of the events scheduled when the archaeological treasures from China were here. She had read the catalogue ahead of time and whizzed around, not missing a thing, looking at the objects with enthusiasm and from her own point of view, not just looking because somebody said this is great, you must see it. There were swarms of friends there and she enjoyed it all, being kind of cool about it, but loving it, signing autographs, having the guards say, "Hello, Miss Cunningham."

Wherever we went she seemed to know people, or if she wanted to know someone, she had no hesitancy in making some little remark that would trigger a conversation. If she heard someone speaking German, or if a person—any kind of person—seemed interesting, she'd zoom right in, and they'd soon be chattering away. Not necessarily on lofty subjects; it could be anything from gardening to kids to poetry. She was never at a loss for ideas, and she was continually spouting—whether she was talking to some aged Chinese about calligraphy or exchanging recipes with a friend, she was committed to the exchange.

She and I used to talk a lot about sewing. She liked to sew and liked good fabrics, Liberty linens and those nice batiks. She wasn't a good sewer in that she didn't spend time on the finishing touches, but she was very aware of the lovely, sensual fabrics she wore. And she was a true recycler. That Marimekko dress she wore on the Johnny Carson show . . . I made it for myself, but it didn't look right and I gave it to Imogen. She loved it. Very vivid colors.

As a grandmother—well, she wasn't the kind who would baby-sit. She announced very forthrightly at an early stage that she wasn't going to. But she was helpful to our daughter Loren as she grew older. Loren was interested in art and enjoyed talking to Imogen about it and looked to her for ideas. And Imogen gave her nothing but encouragement and stood behind her in the different things she wanted to do.

YAO SHEN

Yao Shen, emeritus professor of English linguistics, University of Hawaii

I remember my first impression of Imogen. I was a new student at Mills in 1936, and she came to a reception. I had gone to missionary schools in China and we were taught American songs—Clementine, and her feet were so big that she wore size number nine. My mother had small feet, bound feet. My first impression of Imogen was here is this little American lady with tiny, tiny feet. Of course she was terrifically intelligent. You could tell by the eyes. And she was very straightforward. Whatever came into her mind she would say. That was very beautiful for me, because I am straightforward. Not like my friend in New England who would say when I asked, "Did you enjoy the party?" "Oh, my cheeks hurt from pretending."

Being a foreign student I had no place to go on the holidays and vacations, and Imogen would take me in. She had a huge house in Oakland, and I stayed with her one summer. She was teaching summer school somewhere, so she asked if I would mind cooking for the boys. The boys fixed my breakfast, and I fixed their suppers. Chinese food, and sometimes kind of imitation

American food. They loved it, and we all had the best time. The boys would do the dishes — Imogen raised them well. I only did the cooking.

She didn't have an easy life, but she had no grudge against it. I think she was not happy when they were living in Oakland. I never asked her about it, but she did say to me that as a mother she loved her sons, as a wife she loved her husband. But Roi was not particularly fatherly or thoughtful to his sons.

Imogen took me in as a member of the family, and after I left she always corresponded. She would tell me about her boys — that Gryff was an architect, and he had an engineer friend fix up her darkroom in such a convenient way, and she was so happy to have such a wonderful boy to do this for her. Then Ron was a photographer, and they had so much in common. And Pad was a geologist; he was the last one to get married. She said she hoped he'd get married soon. "I told him, 'Go out and find your own woman. I'm sick and tired of ironing your big shirts!'" She loved to talk about the twins, how they had a special affinity. That they meet in their own

Yao Shen JUDY DATER

way that nobody can touch. They have their own wives and families, but the twins themselves are like a separate unit. She saw that as so beautiful in them, unique.

Imogen photographed me many times, and I've often wondered why. One day I went to her home and she showed me these huge, handsome fans, and she had me sit in the corner with pillows. I asked what I was supposed to do. She said, "You don't do anything, Shen Yao"—she always called me in the Chinese way—"you just talk, just talk." There was a conversation, we really conversed, and she kept on shooting me. Oh, she shot an awful lot at that session. She was capturing my moments.

I never thought of myself as an object beautiful in the eyes of an artist, the way Imogen saw me in that picture with the fans. It never occurred to me that someone would tell me to wear that particular dress, that particular ring, that someone would notice me, the dress, the ring, all three together. I never see myself at such moments. It takes an artist to catch those moments. Rossetti said, "A sonnet is a moment's monument." For a photographer, the photograph is the moment's monument.

I don't know why she took so many pictures of me—every time I saw her. When I came back from seeing my mother in China, in 1948 I think, I stayed with Imogen. I went to her house right after I went through customs—I needed a rest so badly after the twenty-one-day ocean trip. I was sitting on her back porch relaxing, and she quickly went to her lower place and got her camera. That was the picture of me sitting in the bamboo chair on her back porch—that's my favorite. I always feel that's the real me. It was such a moment of relaxation, a very gratifying moment. I had just seen my mother—took her everything she could dream of, including a refrigerator. I had just had breakfast, I was feeling contented in the warm air, and the bamboo chair was so snug. It's a part of China, and Imogen loved that chair too. It was a moment of complete peace with man, with nature.

I had a very frustrating time with Imogen over the chop. She wanted a little seal to use on her prints, but it had to have all kinds of things on it. I explained that often there are only four characters on the seal, and how could I put her whole life, ninety years, in one seal? I meditated a lot, and then one day the idea came to me. I

Yao Shen and Imogen in the kitchen in Oakland, 1938
RONDAL PARTRIDGE

went to the Chinese dictionary—Imogen: *I-mo-gen*. *I:* idea; *gen:* end. But what would I do with the middle syllable? Then I realized that in Cantonese *mo* is "don't have." "Do you have such and such?" "*Mo*"—"No, I don't have any."

So there it was. *I-mo-gen*—idea without end, which is Imogen.

She loved it. We sent it in modern script special delivery to Hong Kong to have it turned into seal writing. And that's the seal the Trust blind stamps on the prints.

Brett Weston JUDY DATER

40

CHAPTER II

Group f/64 &
the Early Photographic Circle

BRETT WESTON

Brett Weston, photographer

To me, Imogen was not a great artist but a great personality, one of the most unforgettable people I've ever known. She made a great impression on me the first time I met her. I was only about fourteen, and I remember vividly her coming down to see my father before he went back to Mexico. That was about 1925, and we were in Tropico then—it's now Glendale, but then it was a tiny village called Tropico. Roi was with her, a very handsome young man, debonair but nice, very serious and scholarly. He'd sit on the bench in Dad's darkroom and eat bananas and read, and Imogen and my father would go out in the garden and photograph the flowers.

Dad and Imogen were quite close as far as photography was concerned. They respected each other and they were equally dedicated, though in different ways. In fact at one point they were doing the same kind of things, like my father's early platinums and fragments of breasts. Now as to which one influenced the other, I don't know. Imogen was a little older, and it's possible she influenced him somewhat, but I don't know.

She and Roi, and my father too, were very "artistic" and bohemian, part of that artistic era of the twenties. And she remained so. I discarded my beret forty years ago, but she was still wearing hers when she died—her fez, you know, her décor. Special garb—that to me is bohemian.

Of course Imogen as a youngish woman was homely as a mud fence—that red hair! It was part of her charm, though. And Dad always had some beautiful gal around. He just appreciated beauty, but Imogen didn't approve.

I saw Imogen and Roi in Santa Barbara during the Depression. They came down in a big Cadillac and took me to lunch. Roi was very serious. "Brett," he said, "be sure to save your money—that's very important." Here I was living on about twenty dollars a month, buying vegetables for a penny each, eating day-old bread, living on

Imogen, 1922 EDWARD WESTON

beans and prunes—and he told me to be sure to save my money! They must have been fairly successful at that point. He had a steady income from Mills, and she was doing portrait jobs for the movie people, so they could afford to take me out for a dollar-fifty lunch, which was something in those days. Imogen borrowed my darkroom that day. She was a pretty sloppy craftsman. I remember her saying that she often got hypo in the developer from working back and forth. It will take a certain amount, but of course that's why we work from left to right, to avoid that. She was hardly the pristine craftsman she should have been.

Imogen has been a definite force and stimulus in the world of photography on the west coast.

Personally, I don't like all of her work, but then I don't like all of my own work either. She did some very fine things, though. That photograph of Dad and Margrethe Mather is charming, romantic. It caught a mood and a moment in time, which is important, but it is not a great and powerful work of art. Her flower forms were extremely fine, though, and probably the best portrait she ever did was the first one of Morris Graves. That was the greatest. But I think her major contribution was in stimulating young people in the way that Stieglitz did. I don't think either of them, Imogen or Stieglitz, is of the stature of Strand or my father. No way. I think they were both catalysts.

WILLARD VAN DYKE

Willard Van Dyke, filmmaker and photographer, former director of the Film Department, The Museum of Modern Art, New York

When I was living in Oakland and Piedmont, I had a high school sweetheart whose father was a photographer. He was a pictorialist named John Paul Edwards, and he knew all the photographers around. At one point, I decided that the only thing that was going to be important in my life, besides the young lady, was photography, so I made up a small portfolio of my work and I wanted to get Imogen's opinion on it. There was a marvelous collection of photographic magazines of various kinds stacked all over the garage John Paul used for a darkroom, so while my prints washed or dried I would go through them, and I had become very familiar with Imogen's work. John Paul called her up and introduced me, and one Sunday afternoon I tucked my portfolio under my arm and went to see her. I guess I was about twenty at the time—that would have made it 1926—and I had lots of golden curly hair, and I was wearing my white shoes with the black saddle across, and white flannels, and a white turtleneck sweater. Imogen looked at the pictures and was very polite, if not very com-

municative, but I had a rather pleasant afternoon. Later, I heard that someone asked her what she thought of my work, and she had said, "Oh, he'll never be a photographer, he's much too pretty."

That was my introduction to Imogen, and we were friends from that time on. There were times when she would let me have her studio for an afternoon if I had a particularly urgent reason— some young lady whose house we couldn't use —and Imogen would conspire to bring this young love affair to a reasonable conclusion. We were great friends. I loved her, and I liked her work, and we got along very well together. That was the last sharp remark I ever heard her make about me. I heard plenty about other people, but I was lucky.

So Imogen and I were friends well before Group f/64 started. That group came about in a simple way. I had a very close friend from college named Preston Holder. Both of us were very art conscious, and one day after we'd been in San Francisco doing the galleries, we started talking about groups of artists that had gotten together—the Fauvists and the Blue Four, and so on. Preston said, "You know, we really ought to get a group of photographers together. There is a kind of western style of photography." And I said, "Yes, it's a great idea. Let's call it U.S. 256." That was because I was using an old rapid-rectilinear lens that used the uniform system. U.S. stood for "uniform system," and 256 was the equivalent of 64, as far down as the lens would stop. Not long after I had a little party at my studio at 683 Brockhurst. Imogen was there, and Ansel Adams, and Edward Weston—and I think Sonia Noskowiak was with him. I broached the idea of the group and the name, and Ansel said he thought it was a splendid idea, but people wouldn't understand the U.S.—they'd think it was for the United States, and 256 could mean anything. Why didn't we call it "Group f/64"? It

was the same number, and the graphics would be nicer.

That was fine with me. I was just interested in all of us exhibiting together. Looking back on it, I realize I must have had an ulterior motive. I was by far the youngest of the group. I needed them, but they didn't need a group. Anyway we agreed, and we were Group f/64, and Lloyd Rollins, who ran the de Young Museum, gave us a show. It was as simple as that. It was never a formal organization except for the announcement of the exhibition, which listed the names of the people who formed the group—the five of us there that night and John Paul Edwards and Henry Swift. Then on the opposite page it said that from time to time other photographers would be invited to exhibit with the group, and listed four more names there. Dorothea Lange

Willard Van Dyke JUDY DATER

wasn't a member, and she didn't exhibit with us. We had enormous respect for her, but we felt that her style and her goals, her whole iconography, were so different from ours that her work just didn't fit. I think she may have been a bit hurt by being excluded. She certainly never showed it, and we remained friends all our lives, but I think there was some feeling.

It was largely a social group, nothing formal. There were no officers and there was just the one exhibition. It was a recognition that we were friends who thought, to a greater or lesser degree, the same way about photography.

I think we were reacting against pictorialism in photography. Of course there is a painterly quality in some of the things we call abstract, and Weston's rocks or his shell or pepper are not that far from O'Keeffe's flowers. But it was a reaction against the manipulation of the photographic image. We felt that it had to be straight. It had to be sharp and clean and absolutely photographic. Ansel and Edward and I were using the new 8 x 10 camera almost exclusively at that point. And there was another thing: we felt isolated out here. We felt there was an eastern establishment that didn't recognize our existence. I think it was no accident that my little gallery was called 683 Brockhurst, like Stieglitz's 291 Madison, and there was a feeling that Stieglitz might have made some gesture in our direction, but he never did.

We learned that Strand didn't think too well of Weston's work, and that made us defensive. In fact, we didn't exist as far as Strand was concerned. Perhaps Strand had a proprietary feeling. He may have felt that he had done the same kind of material first, and that we were imitating. I don't think we were, though. His work wasn't reproduced much. He felt that reproduction didn't do justice to his prints, which indeed were very beautiful—double-coated platinum, and he would wax the surface to give a nice warm glow to the platinum. So I think he may have felt that we weren't really artists, just dabblers imitating him.

As for Imogen, she was always doing her own thing. I influenced Weston and Weston influenced me. My sand dunes were the first sand dunes— before Weston ever photographed sand dunes. Ansel and Edward and I all tried to find our own

way, our own style, but there was a common impulse behind it. But that wasn't true with Imogen. What other artists did didn't matter. It was her direction, her direct experience of the object through the camera that mattered, and she was unconcerned about the kind of quality we were looking for with an 8 x 10 contact print on glossy paper. She didn't mind printing on other kinds of paper, and it wasn't important if the images often weren't all that sharp. It was her unique way of seeing things that was important, and we all respected her for that. She added something very vital to the body of work that was coming out of the group.

That was Imogen. She did what she felt, and there were no explanations or excuses. If someone questioned her about definition, or something like that, she'd reply with a sharp remark. But there was no conflict. Everybody in the group thought that what she was doing was perfectly compatible with what was happening.

No conflict at all—except later on, between Ansel and Imogen. Maybe conflict is too big a word, because Ansel is a gentleman of the old school, and he had a certain attitude toward women that prevented him, I believe, from conflict of that kind with a woman.

But there was something with Imogen. I think she thought he was a little precious about his photography. She felt that Ansel took great pleasure in making discoveries that were really just his own personal discoveries. I mean, you could find the same formula in *Photographic Facts and Formulas*, but somehow when Ansel discovered it, it was *his*. He would show you with joy how it printed, the subtle qualities—and that rubbed Imogen the wrong way. He was the only one she ever made wisecracks about, and certainly that commercial she made of the funeral parlor in Ann Hershey's film was directly related to the Datsun commercial Ansel made for television. It was her private joke. She was always joking with him, and he didn't quite know how to take it.

At one point Imogen had suggested that all of us in Group f/64 take photographs of each other, but she didn't push the idea. It wasn't like her to push things. I think her idea was that when one of us showed up at her place, she'd photograph him, and that eventually we'd all do the same.

She probably did photograph everyone in the end.

I made quite a nice photograph of her. Nice in that it is gentle, a quality that didn't always show. She had stopped in New York on her way back from Europe, and she came by for dinner. We were sitting out in a little court in the back of the brownstone where I lived, and the light was terribly nice, so I got a Graflex and took a picture of her. I like it very much. It's the way I felt about her.

I was amused by her vitriolic quality—it never affected me—but I think it may have been something of a cover-up. I think also it may have grown out of her doing something that must have been very difficult. When she started out, women were not given the kind of breaks that men were given, to put it mildly. And for her to have to carry around that 5 x 7 view camera with a dozen loaded plates on streetcars to do sittings at people's houses must have been galling. She wasn't a militant feminist, but I think all that had an effect, and she may have felt—at least unconsciously—that she might have gotten more of a break earlier if she'd been a man.

The really big thing she did in her life, the really positive statement for herself, was going to New York after Roi told her he would leave her if she did. She was bitter about Roi for a while, but then she found she had become free. She no longer had to be Roi Partridge's wife. He was an etcher of considerable fame, and every year there was an annual with Roi always there among those at the top, and he was collected, and all that kind of thing. Suddenly, Imogen was free of all that. She was able to stand on her own feet, and she earned the great respect of everyone who knew her, and lots of people who didn't know her, just through her photographs.

Imogen and I could always talk freely. During the United Nations conference I was out in San Francisco for several months making the official government film about the establishment of the U.N. One day I took Imogen to lunch, some place on California Street where they had good fish. She had a glass of wine, and she got kind of loose, and she said, "Willard, there's something I've often wondered. Do homosexuals do what I think they do?" I said, "Yes, Imogen." And she said, "Oh, my goodness, that's disgusting!" I never knew what she thought homosexuals did, because she didn't say.

She had to be a little drunk to ask the question. And it had to be somebody she could trust. We'd known each other a long time, and she'd been my confidante in my love affairs. She lived, at least partially, through other people's love affairs. I had a particularly flaming one during the conference with a woman Imogen had introduced me to, and she was just as curious as could be about it. We could talk freely, and she totally accepted it all.

She never talked about any romantic things of her own. I'm pretty sure there wasn't anything after she got divorced. She wasn't terribly attractive physically. Her attractions were quite other things. Her face had a marvelous kind of radiance but it somehow wasn't sexually attractive. I have a suspicion that Roi was the only man in her life.

I never used Imogen in a film. In those years I was working with a camera that didn't record sync-sound, and with Imogen you'd be missing at least a third of what she was doing without sync-sound. But when I left the Museum of Modern Art some of the patrons asked me what film I would like to have in the archives in my name, and I asked for John Korty's film on Imogen. That was an indication of how I felt about her.

ANSEL ADAMS, *part 1*
Ansel Adams, photographer

I met Imogen around 1926 when I was visiting Mills College with Albert Bender. Albert was a great patron of the arts in the San Francisco area, and I used to drive him up to Mills on some of his trips, when he was carrying books as gifts to the library. Roi Partridge was teaching at Mills then, and Imogen was doing some photography for the college.

Then Imogen joined us when we founded Group f/64 in 1932. I'd like to think that that was about the time she really began to realize her creative potential. Her work became more extroverted, she became more aware of the different things others were doing, and that was stimulating to her.

Just after that she had this wonderful opportunity to go back East to take photographs for *Vanity Fair*. She was so thrilled. It was the first chance she had had to really get out into the professional world. Up to this time she'd mostly been doing photographs of girls graduating from Mills and bringing up those three redheaded boys. She was tired of all that, and here was a chance to do something expansive. On that trip she got

to photograph some very important people, and that gave her self-confidence and stabilized her. That was when she did that portrait of Stieglitz, which I've always thought was an absolutely superior job, full of understanding. Knowing Stieglitz, I can imagine the difficulties involved in taking his picture. Stieglitz once told me that he thought Imogen and Anne Brigman were the only two women important in western photography.

I've heard people say that Imogen felt competitive with me. But in fact there was very little we competed on. In the first place, I'm not a portrait photographer, or only a very occasional one. Possibly rather than competitiveness, she may have felt a little resentment over my perhaps more obvious success. I guess I had more shows, more commercial jobs—but I think she didn't

Ansel Adams JUDY DATER

want those anyway. I was just extremely lucky. For one thing, during those bad times in the early thirties Albert Bender was there to help me along. There were plenty of other talented photographers around, but somehow things happened to go right for me. I think my "success" was also tied in with my conservation work. But it was not all that it appeared—I had quite a time making ends meet in those days, just like everyone else.

There was one sore point I remember. In 1931 Mills asked me to do a catalogue for their School of Science. I had just started the year before to try to make my living from photography rather than from teaching piano, and I really needed the money. And I never thought that Imogen considered Mills as exclusively her domain, so I took the job. But it turned out that she was rather put out about it.

Another sore point was my first technical book, *Making a Photograph*, which came out in 1935. I used only one photograph in it that was not by me, and that was Dorothea Lange's *Bread Line*. Well, Imogen was jealous, annoyed that I hadn't included her too. She always felt caught between Dorothea and me; Dorothea because of her feeling for the human side, and me because of my craftsmanship.

I've always had a feeling that Imogen's final print never quite achieved what she had intended. Her printing was extremely uneven. Some had a perfectly gorgeous quality, but some made me feel, "Jesus, what a great pianist—but the piano's not very good!" You know, in the early days she was thrown together with painters a lot, and painters don't worry about photography, especially photographic technique. So Imogen wasn't very exacting about the way she made photographs. She was inclined to be a little sloppy.

She used to say to me, "I don't know why I try to print when you're around." And I'd tell her that it wasn't hard to be a good printer—everybody *should* be. But then I saw her darkroom! The drying racks were of cheesecloth, and they must have been there for years. They were brown! She just said, 'They do look a bit dingy, don't they?" So she had Ron—I think it was Ron—replace them with racks made of plastic fly screen, like those I use. We never talked about

technical matters much, though. She did ask me once what bromide did in the developer—she knew it did *something*. She'd ask simple questions and expect simple answers.

Imogen used to give me a hard time about what she considered my "too-commercial" side. That was probably another legacy of her being around painters so much. She felt I wasn't enough the artist, wasn't following the studio tradition. Art with a capital *A*. She had had some commercial jobs, and I think she didn't trust advertising. So she didn't do commercial work to speak of, just a few portraits. She did make photographs of artists' works, and Albert Bender got her some jobs. In fact he bought photographs from her. He gave me a print of the *Magnolia Blossom*, one of the most beautiful photographs I've ever owned.

In any case, I know she disapproved of that Hills Brothers coffee can that came out about 1968—the one with one of my Yosemite snow scenes on it. She made that very clear. She sent me one of the cans with a marijuana plant growing in it! And then there was the television commercial I did for Datsun. For every test-drive a potential customer took, Datsun would have a seedling planted by the U.S. Forest Service. I thought it was a pretty good idea to get some trees planted, and if you have to have cars, at least Datsuns get good mileage. But Imogen didn't see it that way. I heard about the takeoff she did of it in Ann Hershey's movie, selling grave plots. I can just imagine her chuckling over the idea.

I used to say that Imogen's blood was three percent acetic acid. She seemed to have an acid reaction to so many things, and she could be very abrupt. But she had another side too. I remember the evening that Dorothea Lange told us that her marriage to Maynard Dixon was breaking up. Dorothea came in, took a deep breath, and said, "I'm leaving Maynard." Well, it was a harrowing moment. We were all close friends of both Maynard and Dorothea; no one knew what to say. And Imogen just burst into tears! I would have expected her to be very stoic, to make some pointed remark. But she cried. I think a lot of that "acidity" was put on, and deep down she was really very soft, very emotional.

Mai K. Arbegast JUDY DATER

48

CHAPTER III

Some Old Friends

MAI K. ARBEGAST

Mai K. Arbegast, landscape architect and horticultural consultant

I met Imogen by a fluke. When I was beginning to teach landscape architecture at Berkeley —that was about 1954—I used to go up to the botanical gardens. I noticed a woman with a beanie hat photographing there, and I was intrigued because she was always around the cactus and succulent area, apparently because the forms were so beautiful. We began to talk.

Then I would see her at the meetings of the California Horticultural Society—she was one of the group that founded the society after a terrible freeze back in 1933—and we became friendly. I was collecting material for a book on trees in the city, and she used to criticize my photographs very candidly. It's very difficult to capture the essence of a particular species of tree in a photograph because you can't work like a painter, compiling characteristic parts from various trees and putting them together in one idealized tree. Instead, you have to photograph a typical young tree, a typical middle-aged tree, a typical old tree. It's like photographing people. Imogen understood that very well, and she'd give me tips. But I was reluctant to ask her for advice because I thought, gee, that's her living—she should be doing the photographs.

Our friendship grew from the fact that we both liked plants. She particularly valued my having a good scientific background because I could tell her things. She was like a sponge when it came to learning more about plants. I'd take her to the wildflower show in Marin, and to gardens. We just liked each other and felt comfortable together. I saw her about once a week over the last ten years.

I don't know when Imogen became interested in plants, but when she was at Mills she got to know Professor McMinn, who had done a book on California and Pacific Coast trees. She was occupied by the children, so she investigated the things around her—plants—and it was a release for her. With plants she did a lot of *looking*, never taking her camera out. Her visual perception of growing things was wonderful, and I learned a great deal from her on that. I'd be talking from a scientific point of view—this is in the same family as that, so the flowers have a similar look —and she'd be looking from an artistic point of view, talking about color and form and texture. Plants aren't written about from that point of view, you know, and so most people look at them in a botanical way only. Imogen's way of seeing infected a lot of people, made them look at plants in a different way. I have the feeling that she may have picked up some of this when she was in Germany. The Germans have done a lot of close-up photography of plants, and Imogen was very German in that aspect of her work.

Her plant photographs are terribly scientific, but at the same time, because they are so clear we really get to the heart of the plant, the gutsiness of the flower. She showed the general placement of the leaves in the cactus, or the relationship of the petals of a flower—that's scientific, but at the same time it's beautiful. The line, the way the flower is placed, the lights and darks— that goes beyond what a scientist would see. I wish some of her fine pictures were in botanical texts instead of photographs with the straight scientific approach. A lot of botanists don't see beyond the fact that a flower is beautiful. They don't see it in terms of composition or line.

Imogen would have made an excellent botanist. But botany takes a lot of time and she didn't have it. That was one of the reasons she enjoyed my company, because I filled those gaps in her knowledge that she didn't have time to fill. How long a certain kind of seed remains viable, that sort of thing. We did it casually, while we were talking over dinner.

Imogen's interest in the Horticultural Society sustained her for many, many years. She may have met James West there, or probably earlier at Mills. But in any case he was working at the University of California Botanical Garden during the period she became really interested in plants, and I think he was a very important influence in her life in terms of her appreciation of plants. I've heard that he was actually from a titled German family, but he went about almost in rags, not caring what he ate or where he slept, completely absorbed in the plant world. He eventually disappeared on an expedition to South America. Imogen had a whole batch of letters from him, and she was always trying to decide where to put them, because she thought they were important. Apparently he was very brilliant and imaginative, and his letters had a lot of good information about plants and collecting. He

must have written like a poet because she read them over and over—they were an inspiration to her.

The little garden in front of her house on Green Street was very important to her. Bob Royston designed it, but he came only that one time, and she felt that he never had a real interest in it. She thought that was like having a baby and abandoning it. Perhaps he did come by at times, but one of the reasons I used to visit her was to help with the garden. It was something special I could do for her. We'd spend hours just pruning the clematis and talking about what plant would be good here or there. I brought her a couple of plants of Else Frye Rhododendron. It was named for a childhood friend in Seattle, and it pleased her to have a plant named for someone she knew. Every plant was personal to her, and she cared very much where it was placed in the garden, and how it looked in every season of the year. The funny little plants on the porch, the bougainvillea that was held together with twistings from vegetables, the fig tree, that Mexican mock orange that was rather homely but had such a beautiful fragrance

The garden
at 1331 Green Street, 1950
IMOGEN CUNNINGHAM

as you came up the steps—they were part of her. Bill Hammer was very important to her because he took off the heavy limbs or the dead limbs of the palm trees. I think Imogen felt that Bill and I were kind of caretakers of the garden and she could count on us.

She thoroughly enjoyed flowers, no matter what they were. Once I took her a tire. We were both recyclers, so we recycled it—planted it with marigolds. Yes, really. Sometimes her place looked like a funeral parlor, vases on top of vases, although she considered florist flowers an extravagance. Flowers were special if they were from your own garden. But she had a wonderful childlike delight in any flowers anyone brought, and had to recut the stems and arrange them.

She was always giving me little cuttings, and I still have a number of them in my garden. One of them was a little piece of geranium from Virginia Woolf's garden.

BARBARA AND DAVID MYERS

Barbara Myers, painter and photographer, one of Imogen's favorite models, and her husband, David, filmmaker.

Barbara: Dave and I met through Imogen. One day I was walking up Green Street and saw Merry Renk walking up the hill with a very far-out-looking lady wearing a black cape and a strange hat. I thought as they approached, "Who is that incredible character?" Merry introduced us, and Imogen's first words to me were, "You are my Mayan Indian, I must photograph you." So we had a big photographic session, and when she had the prints ready she put them all on the back of her couch the way she always did, to look at them for a few days. Dave, who was a very good friend of hers, came over one day and saw them and asked who I was. That was the beginning.

Imogen also helped us elope. I was with another guy at the time, so we had to sneak out in the middle of the night, and Imogen came and helped us. I had some great furniture, but Imogen kept saying you can't take this, you can't take that, Dave doesn't have room in his car—so I lost my great furniture. We went to Burbank City Hall to be married, and Imogen was our only witness. She'd brought her camera to photograph us, but she was so excited she forgot to load it. Amazing.

That was in 1953. Imogen photographed me continuously after that. She said in her book that I was the only model she ever had that liked everything.

Dave: Actually, the picture of Barbara that has been reproduced so much, the one Imogen called *The Savonarola Look*, was really quite unflattering.

Barbara: But interesting. I accepted them all because they were interesting in themselves. I didn't care whether I looked pretty. I remember vividly being photographed with the Taiwan leaves. They were beautiful, paper-thin leaves. Imogen had me lying on the floor with the leaves on a huge pane of glass suspended over my head on two chairs, and I was terrified that the whole thing would come crashing down on me. And it went on for hours.

I was modeling for Imogen in the early days of Polaroid. It was very hard to get the film out of the camera then, and I'd be there for hours while she made shot after shot and couldn't get any of them out. Four hours and not one picture. David finally told her that she had to clean the rollers each time.

Dave: She must have burned hundreds and hundreds of dollars worth of Polaroid. She kept saying, "Well, it was sent to me for nothing."

Barbara: One day a couple of years ago she said to me in this astonished tone, "I just saw Ansel on television doing Polaroids, and they just pop out! It's a whole different thing!"

Dave: Imogen tried to be helpful to me in my career. I was actually in the gardening business when I first knew her, but I had been a photographer, and then in the fifties I began making films. I'm sure it was through Imogen's influence that I was hired to do some short films on artists for the San Francisco Museum television show, a rather nice prestige show on Sundays. One of the first I did was of Imogen photographing a group of blind sculptors. I did a short in that series that I later expanded into a film on Ansel, and Imogen did stills for it. I was really touched to see that after all these years she had listed herself in her chronology for *After Ninety* as assistant to David

Myers on his film on Ansel Adams. Touching, and so modest.

Barbara: Because Dave was in the gardening business, Imogen asked his help with a problem she had at Green Street. There was a huge palm tree outside her house, and she wanted Dave to cut the lower fronds down. But he decided it was much too dangerous.

Dave: The fronds are very, very dangerous. They pierce you and give you frightful infections from the bats and rats in the trees. But Imogen had a brilliant solution. It was just before Palm Sunday,

Barbara and David Myers
JUDY DATER

52

so she called the priest at the Greek Orthodox church on the corner, and he came over happily, cut off the fronds, and took them away for Palm Sunday services. Imogen thought she had a great thing going, but the palms hurt him and he got wise and didn't come the next year.

Barbara: That garden at Green Street was terribly important to her, and she was so pleased when someone did a really good trimming job. Imogen was a walking plant encyclopedia. When she saw our black begonia she freaked out—had to have a piece of it, it was so rare, and where had I found it? I had seen it dying in a motel in Carmel, in fact, and I'd snitched two leaves. She went on and on about it because it was so rare, and it was just amazing the way she poured forth all that information on it.

Another thing that charmed me was the way she loved to talk German whenever she had a chance. I was told that she had almost no accent and really spoke quite well. She loved to read books in German too.

One of the most striking things to me about Imogen was her incredible taste. Every time I saw her everything she was wearing was related. Even when she was very old, even when she didn't feel well, her scarf, her dress were related in color. Even when she was lying on that bed and couldn't get up much, she'd wear a pretty scarf every day. She was incredibly attuned aesthetically, and I'm sure it bothered her a great deal that she wasn't gorgeous. She didn't talk about it, but I felt that her aesthetic sensibility was offended by her own looks. But taste is everything, and Imogen through her taste became someone beautiful.

Dave: But she didn't completely accept that. I believe it was very significant in her life that she felt that she was physically unattractive.

I think, too, that after Roi divorced her she was an extremely lonely person. She kept herself running so that she could cover it up, but basically, inside, she was a lonely person. And I've always thought that she never really got over her feeling for Roi.

Barbara: One time just after I'd met Imogen we went to her very early exhibition at Mills, and Roi was there. She came over and whispered cozily in my ear, "There's Roi. Isn't he handsome?" She was starry-eyed, like a seventeen-year-old girl. She was touching, a real romantic, however much she tried to hide it by being sarcastic.

Imogen and her younger sister Paula were terribly fond of each other, but their relationship was amusing. When we were with them, each of them would keep making asides to us about the other one: Paula complaining about Imogen's untidiness, Imogen complaining that Paula was disgustingly neat, and so on. But they adored each other.

There was also a younger brother, Burns, still living. One day Imogen visited him at an old people's home. We left her in the lobby and waited in the car, for ages it seemed.

Dave: Evidently she'd run into trouble. She'd gotten lost in the labyrinth because she wouldn't

The Savonarola Look (Barbara Cannon Myers), 1960
IMOGEN CUNNINGHAM

53

pay attention to the directions. Then she finally came staggering back into the lobby, giving off a stream of unfavorable comments about the place. The manager followed her out the door, saying, "I'm so sorry, Miss Cunningham, I'm so sorry. . . ."

Barbara: I can't believe she's gone. I really thought she'd live to 125. I think she's up there greeting the newcomers and gabbing with all her old friends.

STEPHEN GOLDSTINE

Stephen Goldstine, president of the San Francisco Art Institute

Ansel Adams introduced me to Imogen. It was in 1951 and I was all of thirteen. One day I was with Ansel photographing outside a building on Chestnut Street when an older woman came up. Imogen would have been under seventy then— fairly young, not the Imogen we know—and she was wearing a hat that must have been two feet in diameter. I was working with a view camera, and she told me I was too young to be going around with a big camera like that. She began to joke with Ansel, and finally she told me to call her. A few months went by and I ran into her again in a camera store. This time she asked me to dinner, and this time I went. It may seem odd that I wouldn't have rushed to take this great opportunity, but in fact I had already had a chance of that kind. My father had sent some of my photographs to Edward Weston earlier that summer, and Weston sent back a sweet note praising the pictures and inviting me down. I did go and it was wonderful, and I saw a fair amount of him over the next several years. So I wasn't absolutely knocked out by meeting Imogen.

Anyway, I went to dinner at Imogen's, and she asked me what I liked besides photography— I liked music—and what I was doing in school. Somehow she got the sense that I was not a serious student preparing myself for a good university like Johns Hopkins, or somewhere nice young men went. I was a boy who might get carried away by a hobby and end up like some members of her own family. I might not do the right thing. In a way, Imogen was a

sorority girl. What I mean is that though she rejected a lot of conventions in her life, she also had some conventional expectations. She felt that you should get on the right track early on and apply yourself. Anyway, she took an interest in me, and since she knew I had met Weston, she suggested that my father and I go down with her to see him. And that began a friendship of some twenty-five years. She used to come to dinner at my parents' home, and though she made a great deal of fun of my mother's enthusiasm for Judaism, she had to be there for the Jewish holidays. She'd be there for dinner on Rosh Hashanah, and she always wanted to be included in Chanukah celebrations because the kids were around, and she came to seders for years.

The next summer, the summer of 1952, I went to Imogen's house every day and helped print and prepare stuff for the darkroom, or just went around with her when she photographed. It was a funny sort of apprentice relationship. She never had praise for my photographs, and I learned early on not to come to her for approval. I expected at times to be treated like a peer, and when a photograph turned out very well—as three or four of them did—she'd sort of nod, but I got nothing like the reaction I had had from Weston. The only comments I remember were about a picture I took of a railroad hopper car from between two buildings. I tried to make a full-scale print, which I thought was typical purist *f*/64 photography. I knew it was not a very alive picture, but I thought it was okay. I really had no conception, just an intuitive feeling, of what made f/64 work different from camera club photography. Imogen looked at it. "Where's your person? A picture like that will never interest anyone." That made sense. The formal composition wasn't strong enough to carry the image on its own. But you know, except for a few observations about the dark-room, that was her lesson for the summer.

Imogen was not only the first woman friend I had, she was one of the few people outside the family I was close to at that age. She used to talk to me about things that bothered me at home or at school, and she was very supportive, but she had rather high conventional expectations. She didn't want me to be stamped out of a mold, but she wanted me to achieve things that were conventionally understood as achievement. She was always telling me about the nice, young Wahrhaftig boy who was going to be a lawyer, and how he went on an archaeological dig and took some terrific slides. And I kept thinking he was eighteen and I was only fourteen, and I had taken a photograph that Minor White thought was wonderful. Brett Weston didn't start photographing until he was sixteen, and sixteen to me

was years away. So I felt in a quiet way that I was very prodigious, but Imogen never took notice. She'd tell me how Ron started photographing, and I wanted to know if he was fifteen or fourteen then. I know it seems ridiculous, but it was very important to me because I had always been a terrible student. Then my father gave me a camera, and suddenly I found myself doing something well—better than my father, in fact better than anyone else I knew. And then, probably for obvious psychological reasons, I quit taking pictures entirely when I was fifteen.

Imogen seemed like a friend. It never seemed odd to me that she was so much older. My next friend, a man of forty, was Minor White. I was seeing a lot of him, and Imogen called my mother up and suggested she shouldn't let Stephen go down to Clay Street to see Minor White. And my mother was all upset, and I was screaming at her, "What do you mean I can't see him? He didn't do anything to me!" Imogen didn't come out and say he was homosexual, but she certainly had a flair for upsetting people. The most ghastly news was something wonderful to be wholesaled. Great catastrophe or small, it went out on the wire. The phone was constantly busy.

I really didn't take very many pictures that

*Dinner at
Stephen Goldstine's, 1952*

summer. Of course when you use an 8 x 10 view camera it's a pretty slow process, and I probably took no more than thirty pictures. Her approval would have meant something, but looking back on it, there was something very healthy psychologically in her not taking any stand on what I was doing. She didn't push me in any way, and encouraged me only in the friendliest, most direct way: "Let's try this." "Try it that way." "If you want to take some color pictures, try it on an overcast day." Come to think of it, she never got enthusiastic about anyone's photographs, including her own.

In fact there were a lot of things that were very healthy about my relationship with Imogen. For one thing, I came from an upper middle-class household—far from wealthy, but comfortable—and the amount of money she survived on astonished me. It was regularly under $2000 a year. In those days in the fifties her price for a sitting and five prints was $100 and $5 apiece for extra prints—mounted 8 x 10s! It struck me as remarkable that she obviously didn't want for things. And she didn't acquire stuff, she wasn't acquisitive. She eschewed her father's spiritualism, but on the other hand she was about as unmaterialistic as anyone could be. She didn't want junk around. That didn't mean she had to wear crummy clothes or whatever, but she bought only what she needed, in a very modest way, and craved nothing.

That also influenced the way I lived when I was

Stephen Goldstine JUDY DATER

younger. I became interested in design when I met her. She had an Eames chair, and I saved for months from the jobs I got photographing relatives to buy one of those chairs. And then she introduced me to Jo Sinel, the industrial designer, and he told me about hanging bookcases. So I figured out how to put channels on the studs, and I hung a bookcase. I changed my whole physical environment. Instead of a bed with a headboard, I had a daybed like Imogen's. I got one of my parents' old Oriental rugs, and she gave me the name of someone to fabricate wrought iron legs for a flush-door table—this was before people had doors for tables—and she took me to Jo's studio to get an industrial light to hang from the ceiling with a counterweight. So Imogen changed my environment. She made me realize that one could live modestly, in fact be little short of penurious, and still have a rather rich life. It was a bit like having a living Thoreau in San Francisco, though Imogen used to remind me that Thoreau went into town every night. He didn't stay out there at the pond. He went in and played checkers and talked to his friends. Imogen didn't stay out at the pond either.

For three years after I met Imogen she kept saying I must meet wonderful Ron, crazy Ron, living out there with a greenhouse in the valley. Finally I did meet him, and saw him often over the next fifteen years, and he came to play a quite significant part in my development. I think I've seen more photographs by Ron Partridge that are informing and profound than I have by his mother. Imogen always did tell me that Ron was a great photographer, and I saw what she meant when I saw him working in certain contexts. Send him to a wedding or a party with a camera and he will take more incredible photographs of a situation like that than anybody on the face of this earth. He gets tuned in on different levels to what's going on—it's uncanny. Imogen knew that and collaborated with him on certain things.

Imogen admired Ron's photography, but she showed that conventional expectation thing again there. She always had certain reservations about him because he didn't go to college. We don't see Imogen in the Mom context, but when Gryff was little she was Mom. And in fact she didn't let the family split up until Gryff was

ready for college. He was a couple of years older than the twins, and they had to fend for themselves.

Imogen was a great person and an important influence on my life, but her photographs don't do for me what those of some other photographers do. I remember her talking to me about meeting August Sander and seeing her photograph of him. But when I look at that book on his work I see the map of the nation of Germany laid before me. Imogen's photographs don't do that. They don't reveal the people the way Sander's do, with a kind of power that is uniquely given to the camera. But perhaps that book on Sander was marvelously edited, and perhaps among Imogen's work there are images that will mean a lot to us for centuries too.

I was not Imogen's closest friend by any means, but I knew her well for over twenty-five years. She was still very lucid in the last couple of years, in fact more lucid than at almost any other time. She did a little television spot to promote the educational station KQED. Just a little thirty- or forty-second spot, but it had a kind of uncanny directness with charm that is given to few poets at any age. In a few moments she was able to say why she had been born and why you should be interested in public television. She came across as a gifted and caring person, without any cuteness, in a way that perhaps no other celebrity in the region could have done.

She was a celebrity. It's funny, she and Ansel were always important in photographic circles, but those circles used to be much narrower than they are today. Then suddenly she and Ansel are not only celebrities, but probably about as recognizable as anyone you can name in the Bay Area. It has a lot to do with how seriously photography has come to be taken, not just the art form, but the whole photography world. It all happened in the late years of Ansel and Imogen. Stieglitz is long dead. Weston, Steichen, Evans, Strand are dead. But Imogen was to the end, and Ansel still is part of a living force. They brought identity and life to photography, and in a way made it news. So everybody in photography is indebted to them for the role they played.

Morley Baer JUDY DATER

CHAPTER IV

The Photographers

MORLEY BAER

Morley Baer, photographer

During the war I met a guy named Horace Bristol, who'd been a *Time* photographer in San Francisco. He told me that if I ever went to California there were two people I had to see: the Papa and Mama of all photographers out there, Edward Weston and Imogen Cunningham. I didn't really understand at first. I said, quite seriously, "I didn't know they were married." "Oh, no," he said, "they're the spiritual Papa and Mama."

Well, my last job in the Navy took me to San Francisco, and while I was there I went to Carmel. I was taking some photographs of a new shop in the Pine Inn. One of them was a display in a window facing the street. I set up the camera and as I was looking through the ground glass a funny little face appeared. An elderly woman and a tall young man were standing at the window, and I knew if I waited long enough they would go away. So I walked around in front of the camera and then noticed some dust on the lens and blew on it. Suddenly there was a sharp knock on the window and the little woman was saying something I couldn't hear. So I went to the door and she snapped, "Don't blow on your lens, young man!" "My god," I said, "you must be Imogen Cunningham!" "I am, what's it to you?" She looked and acted just the way Bristol said—you know, that face and the white hair and the vinegar tongue.

I hated saying it while she was alive, but at first I wasn't particularly drawn to her photographs. I liked the *Magnolia Blossom* and the early flower things very much, but until I had seen a lot of the portraits I couldn't understand why she liked the ones she showed so often. They seemed very offbeat. I wondered why she

didn't do things more in keeping with the fact that she was an old lady. Of course that wasn't Imogen at all—she still had such a young spirit. I remember once when she came to talk at the Art Institute she brought a pack of photographs and sort of strewed them about. Edward Weston handled prints with grace and delicacy, but she was careless with them, and I thought maybe they didn't mean much to her. That may have put me a bit off the first portraits I saw, because they were just unmounted, crudely printed 8 x 10 prints. And there seemed to be no contrivance or control of what was going on in them. But when you put a lot of them together and studied them, you saw that there was a kind of control that most good photographers have, control that looks like no control at all.

She showed the students a group of photographs she had made in Europe, I think in Germany. I remember when she was getting ready for that trip she was all excited about it and full of fun, and said she was going to take photographs of people and subways and street-cars and all that because she wanted to see what they looked like in comparison to those she knew so well in this country. There must have been fifty or sixty of these photographs. The students liked them, but I couldn't see any connection between them, any kind of control, any incisive quality as to character, to place and time. I saw those photographs several times, and the third or fourth time they had been culled down. Somebody had done a wonderful editing job, and there were eight or ten that suddenly assumed great incisiveness both as to individuals and place. You might not have thought of Germany immediately, but you sure knew it was Europe and you sure knew these were lower middle-class people. You knew they felt free, open to the person handling the camera. I remember one of a rather fat man. I don't know even now if he was a butcher, but boy, if ever I saw a butcher at ease in a chair, it was that man! But all this came only after seeing the same photographs several times.

I had a delayed reaction to the photograph of Morris Graves too. I knew Graves's work fairly well, and when I first saw Imogen's picture of him, the early one, I couldn't understand how it could be taken as a definitive portrait. Now I admit openly, was I wrong! The more I found out about Morris Graves, and I found out a great deal about him over the years, the more I realized what a tremendous portrait it is. It has a feeling of mystery in it, it evokes the kind of atmosphere that you find in Graves's work — his birds have that sense of mystery. I don't know if that's his own garden or some place Imogen found in the northwestern forest, but she got a light, a perspective, a scale between his figure and the background that has a kind of mystery, an oriental quality that recalls his work rather than just defines his features. That picture made me realize what tremendous insight Imogen had about people and what they stood for.

I think it was the sheer numbers of photographs I saw of hers that began to make me see the relationships between them and see in them many things I hadn't seen before. Fifteen or twenty years ago you didn't see many of Imogen's photographs — Edward's and Ansel's were all over the place, but Imogen was really an unknown quantity — and I didn't really see the direction in her work until I'd seen a great deal of it.

At first I also thought that Imogen wasted the time of the people in the classes at the Art Institute. She never said a definite thing about photography in her life that I know of, and in the classes she sort of ruminated about her own way of working and what it meant to live where she did. She'd brag a bit about having some movie mogul call her up in the middle of the night or something like that, but I never heard her say one thing about making a photograph that anyone would write down and take

away. But the students were enthralled by her. Perhaps it was in contrast to Dorothea Lange, who had absolutely no sufferance for fools and scared the hell out of them. But Imogen would come in and ramble through her mind — no direction, no control, it seemed. But her appearance, her manner, her voice, her anecdotal recall induced a good feeling. She just walked back and forth, talking, like an actor on the stage who knows every bloomin' board and is so graceful and well trained that you can't see the wheels work. Now I'm not saying Imogen was an actress, but just that there was no sign of contrivance or control in her manner or her photographs, at least not in the last few years. Boy, people loved her! The women especially, long before the feminist movement, felt she was a kind of lodestar.

Imogen had a genuine feeling of support for the working photographer. She was a member of the ASMP [American Society of Magazine Photographers], and of course she realized that she was very different from the average member, but she'd say, "I'm just another working photographer. People hire me to do portraits, and I go do portraits." And you realized it was not only funny, it was true. She wanted to know what the other members were doing, and she was no outsider at the meetings. I remember Imogen getting to her feet and putting in her two cents worth about the most mundane things ASMP people talk about, just as if she were running a studio in San Francisco or working for ad agencies.

During the late forties and fifties when I was in Carmel, Imogen used to come down to see Edward Weston occasionally. I had gotten to know Edward well, and I would see them together. They were very genuine colleagues, with a real regard and love for each other.

I like a lot of the work being done today, but it doesn't have the kind of personal viewpoint that you feel in the work of Edward and Ansel Adams and Imogen.

We talk glibly of the spirit continuing after people go, and there's no doubt about it in my mind. It not only goes on, it mushrooms and bursts all over the place in all kinds of people. I'm not pretending that my own work is influenced by Imogen, but nevertheless, as an individual—her feeling for life, the closeness that went into her relationships, the way she talked and acted—she left a mark on me. I don't know how, or if I'll ever use it, but I sure can't deny it. Edward Weston and Ansel Adams —and Ansel is still alive and vigorously kicking— and Imogen are a triumvirate of heroes. There just aren't any more like that.

RONDAL PARTRIDGE, *part 2*

I worked quite frequently with Imogen, especially in the last ten years of her life. Sometimes she would give me the job to do, sometimes we would do it together. I sort of enjoyed it, and I never had any trouble about competing with her. We never competed.

Most of my life I did not think of Imogen as more than just a good photographer and a great personality. At least that was my estimate of her until her show at Stanford in 1967, her first big retrospective. I walked into that show and saw the whole circle of all my mother's work, and I stood there and I said, "Wow! I've been underestimating her all my life!" At that moment I understood what Imo was all about.

I know it sounds incredible, but it isn't really. Remember, I was brought up on the stuff. I held the lights on those people.

Of course Imogen influenced me. I remember at the age of four or five running out and picking up at her command the sun prints, the printing-out paper she used for all her proofing for years. And when I was about five and a half, I was given the responsibility—and was very proud of it—of judging the density of the proofs. I was interested in printing—it still seems a miracle to me—and I used to stand on an apple box turned on end to look into my mother's sink, so I must have been very young.

I was only about sixteen when I started working for Dorothea Lange. Dorothea and I became very close; her family became my family. Dorothea and Imogen were friendly, but they were never really very close.

Imogen didn't know anything about technique, and she didn't seem concerned about it. She used any developer anybody told her to use. Of course, just the other day I was saying that she was never concerned about things like the Zone System— but that's not true. I've seen a negative of hers filed with one of Ansel's sheets with all the figures marked à la Zone by Imogen. A treasure. But the negative is terrible. Imogen's negatives are worse than ones developed by amateurs in amateur darkrooms. Many are on the edge of non-usability.

Almost every negative she ever printed has a yellow stain on it. She'd rub a print between her palms to bring the highlights down, she'd wipe her hands off on a towel, and then—with her hands still full of developer—take the negative out of the enlarger and put it in the envelope. All those yellow spots!

Imogen never talked about photography, or what she was planning to do, or where she was going to do it. She just did what was in front of her. Someone would drop into her studio and she'd say, "Sit down, I'll photograph you." And the negatives were so bad that she used only about one percent of them. Except for the double exposures. She had an infallible sense about the double exposures. She probably used two-thirds of them.

So she didn't plan, she didn't previsualize—at least not apparently. What she did was take a great many photographs and select the best. People aren't fully aware of that ability of hers to recognize something that was very good. Her *Magnolia Blossom* is great, but she made a hundred magnolias—literally one hundred negatives of magnolias—that she threw away. When we were kids we used to throw her rejected negatives into the fireplace—the nitrate would explode— hundreds, thousands. God, how I wish we hadn't!

I think Imogen's portraits are some of her best work. That double-exposure portrait of James Broughton, *The Poet and His Alter Ego*—a fine concept. And the one of Morris Graves is perfectly beautiful. She knew how to home right in on the personality of the sitter with very little fuss or bother.

I'll never forget the day she came down to Carmel to take my picture for *People* magazine. That was in March 1976. I thought she'd be there for just an hour or so, so I'd planned a very busy schedule for the rest of the day. But Imogen breezed in about ten in the morning, gave me a kiss, and announced, "Ansel, I'm here to take your picture and you are to take mine, and I'll be around for as long as it takes—two or three days if necessary." There was no point in arguing with Imogen once she had made up her mind, so there went my plans. And she already knew where she wanted to take the picture. "Ansel,

Imogen and Ansel Adams, Carmel, 1975
ALAN ROSS

what's that place where you keep your negatives?" "Oh, you mean my vault." "Yes, that's the place for your portrait." She used to kid me about being the only photographer with a vault for his negatives. I guess I do have a sort of California earthquake mentality, but maybe that's from having lived through the San Francisco earthquake in 1906. Anyway, she had me sit on a ladder in front of the ivy-covered door to the vault, and then took one of me sitting on the steps by the front door. She said she liked that one because it showed my crooked nose. I broke it during the 1906 earthquake when I fell down on the coping of our front walk during the after shock. They were good pictures she made that day.

That was the last time I saw her. The last time I talked to her was just a couple of days before she died. I asked her how she was. "Awful. I don't know why they keep me alive in this lousy world." "Come on, Imogen, it isn't that bad. There's your work and everything." "But I'm so dizzy, I can hardly stand up." "Well, you are standing, aren't you?" "Yes, I am, in fact." Then we talked a lot of nonsense and gradually she got brighter, and at the end of ten minutes she was chipper as all get out.

I think Imogen was really very lonely. She had all those people around her and working with her, but she really needed someone to live with her and keep her spirits bright. Georgia O'Keeffe has a wonderful young man named Juan Hamilton who keeps her going with his kidding and attentions. He introduces her as "a viper, the rattlesnake of the Pecos." And O'Keeffe just laughs. I always wished Imogen had had a friend like that.

ARNOLD AND AUGUSTA NEWMAN

Arnold Newman, photographer, and his wife, Augusta

Arnold: I did a story once for *Holiday* on San Francisco, covering people, food, restaurants, everything. For the cover I scouted locations and finally decided to photograph a whole bunch of people in front of a cable car on the big street on top of Nob Hill. We had policemen, museum people, workers, a couple who just happened to be walking by, all sorts of people—and, of course, Imogen. We had to assemble this crowd in front of a cable car in a few minutes, then disassemble them, then reassemble them when another car came by. It was one hell of a thing to put together. As it turned out, it was a drizzly day, but we had to go ahead. So we got the group assembled, and then Imogen absolutely stole the show: she announced she was going to put her umbrella up. And there she was, dead center with this bright red umbrella. It was delightful and amazing, and it made the photograph—as she knew it would.

I always used to visit Imogen whenever I was in San Francisco. We'd usually wind up at dinner, sometimes with a whole crowd of people, talking into the wee hours. One time I was in town doing some food stories for a series for *Look* magazine. The food editor was dying to meet Imogen, as everybody was, so we went over to Green Street. Imogen swept her off her feet. She announced she was going to write a cookbook one day on how to make meals with canned foods, and with that she prepared what seemed like a gourmet meal for us out of things she just had around the house. I could see the editor's mind working away, thinking we ought to do a story about Imogen, and in fact when she got back to New York she kept wondering why we hadn't done it while we were out there. Eventually we did go back and do it. Imogen was very patient, marvelous to photograph. Most photographers are very patient subjects, because they know

Arnold and Augusta Newman JUDY DATER

what the photographer is going through.

I've always regretted not having done a really great portrait of Imogen. I photographed her half a dozen times, but I haven't made any really good prints. Maybe it's like photographing members of my own family—I just can't do well with them. And Imogen put me off, you know—in a photographic sense she terrified me. I'd think if I didn't do a good job she'd think I was a terrible photographer, though of course she'd never actually have said that.

I imagine she was rather grateful for all the attention that was paid her toward the end. Like Man Ray, who had been sadly neglected for a long time by both the art and photography worlds, she had felt hurt about being a bit left out. A number of times she said, "Oh, we've done all that, and somebody comes along and imitates us, and everyone thinks he's a genius!"

She started very young when there were a few women photographers, but most of them were photographing very daintily, while Imogen was doing really serious photography. Nice girls didn't do that, but she used to say, with a gleam in her eye, "But then I wasn't a nice girl." She believed that a woman should do everything, that there shouldn't be any barriers, but she really didn't like the feminist movement. Why have a movement? Women are as good as men, and she didn't have to join a movement to prove herself. If she could make it, then any woman can.

Augusta: I wish I could have seen more of Imogen. I saw her mostly in New York, and that wasn't often because she didn't like New York—the crowds, the noise. Of course she didn't travel much in her later years. I remember at the time of the winter Olympics in Japan—she was about eighty-nine then—the committee wrote asking her to go to Japan to photograph the Olympics—in the snow. She said dryly, "I told them I couldn't quite make it."

Arnold: To me, Imogen is one of the giants of photography. We have a number of her prints hanging. The one of the hairpins on the bed—that was a school assignment. She said that if she gave her students an assignment, she thought she'd better show them she could do it too. And the portrait of Morris Graves—that to me is one of the great landmarks in portraiture. She didn't just take someone out into the woods and photograph him. She wedded the whole thing—the setting, and who he is and what he is—and so it all works beautifully together. Those two photographs are so different, and yet they are both so absolutely Imogen. She could do a lot of things and do them beautifully, but it was all her.

In the kitchen at Green Street
JAMES G. FRIEDMAN

LAURA GILPIN AND DAVID DONOHO

Laura Gilpin, photographer, and David Donoho, photographer, retired teacher of photography at San Jose State College

Laura: With Imogen gone I'm now the senior photographer of our kind of photography. I don't know of anyone older. I don't welcome the mantle, but maybe I'm not going to pass it on for a while. I don't get around the way I used to, but Thursday we're going to fly up to Shiprock to photograph. Then I want to fly over the Canyon de Chelly again when the leaves have turned, and then follow the valley clear down to where it joins the San Juan River. I should have started this book on the canyon thirty years ago.

I'm not proud of my years yet. There's so much I could have done and should have done, but I was just too busy earning a living.

Photography seems to be a profession that fits women very well. I've always admired Julia Margaret Cameron's work, and of course I knew Gertrude Käsebier very well. In fact it was through her that I went to the Clarence White

Laura Gilpin JUDY DATER

School in 1916. I knew of Imogen's work way back then, but in fact I didn't meet her until about twenty years ago. She was a terrific individual, and her work had great individuality. She knew what she was doing.

David: Imogen told me once that she saw some photographs of Käsebier's and said to herself, "I want to be just as good as she is." It was after that that she went to study in Berlin.

Laura and Imogen worked productively in the twentieth century longer than any other two photographers. One of the most graphic things I ever heard Imogen say was when she was about eighty-five or eighty-six. "It really bugs me," she said, "to see these old ladies sitting around on porches in rocking chairs. They act like they're ancient, and I'll bet they're not a day over seventy! They say things like"—and she put on this quaking old voice—"'Oh, Imogen, how do you manage to keep so busy?' And I'd look at those old girls and I'd say, 'I don't *manage* to keep busy. I *am* busy.'"

Imogen suggested we exchange photographs once. She did quite a bit of that. So I chose the portrait of Stieglitz in front of the O'Keeffe painting. "David," she said, "that's going to be a valuable print. Do you see that sticker on the back? It says that that print was submitted for the 'Family of Man' show at the Museum of Modern Art—and that it was rejected."

She took that photograph at An American Place in 1934. "It was quite an experience," she said. "You see that expression Stieglitz has on his face? He looks as if he didn't like me. Well, he didn't. It was really unforgettable. I had to borrow his 8 x 10 camera, and it was such an old rickety-rackety wooden job that after I put in a holder I had to wait at least a minute for the thing to quiet down before I could make an exposure."

Laura, do you remember that autograph I brought you? Imogen's photograph of her hands?

Laura: Oh yes, of course. "By the hand of Imogen to Laura Gilpin, with long memory and love."

PIRKLE JONES AND RUTH MARION BARUCH

Pirkle Jones and Ruth Marion Baruch, photographers

Ruth: We came to know Imogen when we were at the California School of Fine Arts in the late forties. She was always very hospitable to us. Her house was always open to us, she was quick to serve us a fine meal, and she enjoyed our work. She was especially kind to me at one time. I was very ill, mentally ill, in a hospital in Napa, and I didn't hear from many people. We weren't really close to Imogen, but she sent me a bottle of 4711—it's a German cologne, you know. She knew I was from Germany and she thought it would make me feel better. I was very touched by that.

Pirkle: That was one of her fine qualities. She always thought of a person as an individual, and

no matter how simple a gift was, it was always tailor-made. People were her hobby—she wasn't totally centered on photography—and she knew hundreds and hundreds of people. It was phenomenal. It took a special person to deal with that many people all the time.

It's interesting how many professional people Imogen knew. Many psychiatrists, many other doctors, many architects. She could speak with intelligence on a great many subjects. How she kept up with all this information is beyond me.

Ruth: I felt she really wanted to be closer friends with us, but somehow I didn't quite respond. Of course we happened to be very close to Dorothea Lange—I just felt closer to Dorothea as a person. Perhaps it was because Imogen didn't have the great social conscience Dorothea had, or probably it was because of Imogen's sharp tongue. She was extremely sharp. Edward Weston got a kick out of it, and Ansel was very fond of her. But Dorothea said she had had reservations about her at first, until she realized that Imogen had an inferiority complex. I sensed that too, and I grew to like her better as the years went on.

She mellowed in time, and she was always nice to me. In fact she went out of her way, and she always treated me as a professional equal, which I thought was beautiful. She was very generous in that way.

Pirkle: I think the fact that Imogen had been through the struggle of a woman in the profession undoubtedly had some bearing on that. She wasn't a crusader on that subject, but because she knew so many people and became so well known and respected, she could have some influence on that and on other things. She became a public figure, and people would ask her to be on committees. For instance, I was in a group some

*Pirkle Jones
and Ruth Marion Baruch*
JUDY DATER

years ago to stop the freeway being built through the Panhandle and Golden Gate Park. Imogen was on the board of that committee and took a very definite public stand—despite her friendships for people on the other side, like Lawrence Halprin. She met him head-on in some of the public meetings. There was nothing apolitical about her there, or of course on the subject of the Vietnam War.

Ruth: We didn't really know Imogen's family, though we saw something of Ron. He was very friendly with Dorothea Lange, almost a family member. I think in a way Imogen wanted to be independent of her family, she wanted to do her work. She had raised her kids—and she probably had quite a struggle doing it—and now it was time for them to do their own things. Now Dorothea in her later life wanted to have all kinds of family gatherings, but Imogen was glad to have the family gone and to have her freedom. She visited them and had certain responsibilities, but she refused to let them consume her. Still, when she was arranging her final affairs she made provisions for the family by setting up the Trust. The tight family thing was still there.

One time I was asked to write a criticism of Imogen's work for a magazine, but I refused. I wouldn't criticize a colleague, and Imogen wouldn't have either. She's not my favorite photographer, but she's done some very, very fine things. Her plant things are exquisite. And it was admirable the way she would try different things, tried to free herself. I mean, she was working mostly within the tradition of Group $f/64$, but she would try a little of everything—somewhat documentary things, like the two youngsters in the coffee house or the environmental portraits.

Pirkle: The city had some effect on her work. Not that she did many pictures that were purely San Francisco, though she did work a bit in the Haight-Ashbury. She wasn't deeply interested in doing photographic essays. It was the visual things that struck her. That was true with people too. She'd see someone rather exotic or striking, and she'd ask the person to come for a sitting. I think the purely visual appealed to her more than the content. She probably would have made the same kind of portraits if she had lived in New York, but it would have been harder for her.

Ruth: She wouldn't have been as comfortable in New York. San Francisco's a friendly place. She liked having her plants around her, and her garden. I think it would have been much harder for her to have been accepted and loved in New York the way she was in San Francisco.

CHRIS JOHNSON

Chris Johnson, photographer, teacher at California College of Arts and Crafts

I first met Imogen at the opening of the big Ansel Adams show at the San Francisco Museum of Modern Art in 1972. I was wandering around looking at the work, feeling a bit out of place with all those important art people, when I saw this strange little old woman escorted by a tall, handsome young man. She was dressed in black from head to toe, with a large black hat with a veil hanging down to her chin and black stockings and shoes, as if she were at a wake. She'd go up to a photograph and lift her veil to look at it and kind of shake her head disapprovingly and then go on to the next. I had heard of Imogen Cunningham and I knew it was she, but you'd have been drawn to her just by the odd way she was acting. Well, I went over and I introduced myself very nervously. "Who are you?" she said, very directly, as if to throw me off balance. I told her I was a photographer. "Oh no, not another one! What else do you do?" I told her I also managed a natural food store. She thought that was better. She could talk about buying salt-free bread and establish a line of communication between us while she found out who I was. I was amazed that she was even taking the time to talk to me, but suddenly she said, "I want to photograph you. I like your hair." I was flabbergasted, but I agreed to call her. Eventually she did photograph me, but that never was the basis of our relationship. We were friends.

A couple of years later I asked her why she was dressed that way that night. She said she had done it to rib Ansel. He was all decked out in his red blazer and white collar and she wanted to give some comic relief to his seriousness. And it was funny. There was Ansel standing tall and grand, and there was little Imogen dressed like a mourner, as if to say that she didn't take her work or herself all that seriously, but she knew that she was just as important and that her work was just as meaningful. Oh, she ribbed Ansel a lot, but she truly respected him.

I often felt unsure about my relationship with her. I'd show her a new photograph and she'd

Chris Johnson JUDY DATER

never be very positive. She'd point out something that was wrong with it and talk about the area in which I needed to grow. Because her opinion mattered so much to me, that always kept me a little off balance. In fact she liked me, but sometimes I'd let my insecurities keep me from calling her for a month or two and then she'd call and say, "Why haven't you called me? Aren't we still friends?" Her message to me was: grow up. And as I grew more, as our relationship developed and I became more confident, she responded by sharing more of her life with me. I miss her a lot.

She finally did photograph me. One day while we were talking she got this devilish look in her eye and got up to get her camera. Keeping her eye on me, she moved around and started shooting. She made a negative of me with the light streaming through her shutters across my face and my hair blown up. It ended up as that print of me with the leaf, and just the other day I found out what had happened. She had developed the roll, decided that she liked a certain frame, and while tearing off the leader accidentally tore the last frame right in half. When she made the contact sheet she decided that the torn frame was the best, and she went ahead and made a print. That was typical of Imogen. She wasn't the least bit self-conscious about the fact that it was torn. Sometime later she got the idea of putting one of those desiccated leaves across it, with the main stem covering the tear. Somehow it all came together, the idea of the organic leaf, the light going across my face—primal, a great image.

I'm still compulsive about negative flaws, but she often used flaws as a way of making a better image. That ease with one's own mistakes, the openness to turn those mistakes into art were really inspiring to me.

Don't be concerned about making mistakes, don't be concerned about what people say or

Chris, 1972 IMOGEN CUNNINGHAM

think about you—there's a joy and power in that attitude, and it's infectious. It's difficult to recognize that attitude in the body of Imogen's work because the images she's best known for are those idealized forms. They express one aspect of Imogen's personality, but you have to look at the mistakes as well as the perfections. That photograph may not be perfectly sharp from one corner to the other, but it's beautiful, it gets its message across, the spirit is there. That was Imogen.

LEO HOLUB

Leo Holub, photographer, senior lecturer in art at Stanford University

That picture of Helena Mayer with her mask and foil is the first photograph by Imogen I recall seeing. I met her in 1939, about the time she took the picture, through Jo Sinel, who was in fact squiring Helena around. Then in the fifties I was a member of an organization called Telesis, a group of architects and planners who were trying to make the Bay region aware of the growth problem. Most of the members were in their twenties or thirties, but typically Imogen was a member too—she always preferred young people, it seemed to me. Well, I didn't see much of Imogen until 1966, when I called her to ask for a print of a photograph she had taken of a Telesis picnic. She couldn't find the negative, but I did ask her to photograph my eldest son, Michael.

She took a liking to Michael, and he started doing odd jobs for her: gardening, trimming the trees, and so on. One day she stood him up against a wall and photographed him—but her Rolleiflex skipped a beat and the negatives overlapped. That didn't bother her, though, and it still makes a fine print.

She sensed an ambivalence in Michael. She talked to him, she understood him. And at the end of a photographic session, she'd say; "Now turn your head during a one-second exposure." She made more than one set like that. From the session with him in his Navy coat, there's one head on and one with the head turning. "One says Michael yes, and one says Michael no." She sensed that ambivalence about my boy—it's "Michael as Steppenwulf."

A couple of years later Imogen had a show at the Smithsonian and then took a trip across Canada. She was gone for two or three months, and while she was away my son Michael shot himself. He was a suicide. Imogen didn't know about it until she returned, and then she wrote me a note saying, "I knew Michael was not making it, and I didn't do my part." She had nothing to do with it really, but because she had sensed the problem that's how she felt.

I drove Imogen down to Stanford when she photographed the director of the Center for Advanced Study in the Behavioral Sciences. The first director had been photographed by Ansel Adams, and they wanted Imogen for Mr. Wilson, the second director. Actually we went down twice—she didn't get the picture she wanted the first time—in my old wooden 1948 station wagon. When you had Imogen in that car someone would turn and point at nearly every block, "Look, there's Imogen!" We went to the director's home, and Imogen photographed him in his house and in his garden using the technique I suppose she used all her life. She had me hold up a piece of black velvet behind him to get a plain background. She chatted in a relaxed way and photographed at the same time. Mrs. Wilson and I were both there, but it was just between Mr. Wilson and Imogen. She was using the Rolleiflex she'd had for so many years, and by this time she used an extra magnifier on top for close focusing.

It wasn't until about a month before she died that I realized she was failing—physically. She never failed mentally. Around the holidays that last year, she sent some jars of jelly and jam with a note for my wife:

Note to Florence: Everything in my house has a story. The marmalade that I have promised to all my friends turned out to be syrup. The little jar marked "Travaglio's Grape" was made from a bunch of very withered and too-long-on-the-vine grapes that my neighbor brought me. The "CBS Jelly" was made for the photographers of CBS, and I was photographed by them while making it. The base (this is for Leo) was that juice he insisted on giving me at Calistoga, plus a bottle of commercial Concord grape drink from the store. The "Sacramento Apricot Jam" is made from a jar of cooked but unsweetened apricots that two farmers in Sacramento sent me.

I still have two of those little jars with her typed labels up on my desk as pencil holders.

I had Imogen come down to Stanford to talk to my classes. That year we had a grant for three speakers, so naturally I hired Imogen. She was there for about three hours, standing, sitting, walking around giving individual critiques, answering questions. We had a full house and it was a thrilling day for all of us, and she found it stimulating too.

In the winter of 1970 she talked to a University of California extension class. There were about fifty people there and she made comments on their work, but she never said do this or do that. I wrote down some of the things she said to the group that afternoon:

A man said he was from Rio Vista, and she said, "Did you ever photograph the postmistress there?" "No." "You should. She doesn't like it."

Someone had jiggled a print in the enlarger. "I love these experimenters, because I think something is

Michael as Steppenwulf IMOGEN CUNNINGHAM

now, and it's sad when one more goes. That sense of character came out of the nineteenth century, I think, the frontier. Those people had a kind of gusto and spirit, and allowed others their idiosyncrasies, and that—the idiosyncracy—to me is always the flavor of a person's soul. In a way Imogen was a frontier woman. She'd have nothing to do with sit-around culture and meditating.

She was a no-nonsense girl in that respect. I remember running into her just a couple of years before she died. She came swinging up that steep hill at the corner near Saint Francis Hospital. I had been to see a doctor, and I said, "Okay, Imogen, now it's your turn to go in." "Don't be silly," she said, "can't I go for a walk? Race you to the corner!" So we raced down the block. In fact she darted off so fast that it was pretty much of a tie. And she was over ninety.

I wrote a poem for her ninetieth birthday:

Imogen and Grover Sales in James Broughton's film,
The Bed, *1967* DEBORAH SMITH

EVERYTHING IS CONNECTED
For Imogen Cunningham's 90th Birthday

The egg is in the star
the star is in the thistle
the thistle is in the spider web
and the wind is in the whistle.

The milk is in the cloud
the cloud is in the puddle
the puddle is in the bullpen
and the cow is in the cuddle.

The sea is in the fish
the fish is chickenhearted
the chicken is in the henhouse
and the egg is where you started.

The idea that someone of ninety has been in and out of all the metamorphoses, you know. She was tickled. "I suppose it's a compliment, calling me a fish!" "Well, Imogen," I said, "the egg is in the star. You know, you're a good egg." "You mean cracked," she said.

PEG FRANKEL

Peg Frankel, friend

My friendship with Imogen was ninety-nine percent lunch and doing errands afterward. I drove a Jeep, which intrigued her, and we'd ride around town doing errands and occasionally we'd go to an exhibit, but nothing more frivolous than that. Aside from fixing lunches, making jellies and jam, and working in her garden, the only things she would give time to were work oriented, right up to the last moment.

Much of what I learned about photography was from going to shows with Imogen. She wasn't analytical, and if she didn't like a photograph, she quickly turned her back on it. And in some areas she had very mixed feelings—about nudity, for instance. Even though Imogen was probably the first woman to photograph male nudes, for her there were nudes and nudes. She drew a line somewhere, but just where I'm not certain. Those early photographs of her husband on Mount Rainier were fairly natural things—though I don't imagine he was really swimming in that cold lake up there. Of course, sitting on the ice

Peg Frankel JUDY DATER

could have been Imogen's idea. There was a bit of the clown in her.

I had known Imogen a long time before I owned any of her photographs. Then I thought I'd better do something about that. Since I did a little book collecting I wanted her portrait of Gertrude Stein; and since I'd always been interested in modern dance and had gone to Bennington when Martha Graham was teaching there, I wanted one of her images of Martha. So Imogen got out her Graham file for me, and I flicked through it, stopping at a photograph of Martha with her torso bare except for a beautiful piece of fabric draped over one shoulder. One arm is over her head, and on the arm are two flies. I thought it was terrific, but Imogen immediately turned it over and said, "You can't have that." "Why not?" "Because it's not nice. I remember the day well. Martha was rehearsing in front of a barn, it was a hot day, and the barn smelled, and those flies were buzzing around." The associations were negative. "I don't like it, and I don't think Martha would either. You can't have it."

I saw another interesting one of Martha's feet, but finally I settled on a double image of her head. Weeks went by and I was beginning to wonder if I would ever see the photographs, until one day after lunch Imogen announced that they were ready. They were on a chair she had next to the door she used for finished business—books and magazines she had borrowed and read, things to be mailed, completed orders. So I took the package and when I got home there were three prints instead of two: Gertrude Stein, the double image of Martha, and those feet. I've gotten very fond of those feet, but I still wanted the torso with the flies, and I brought it up again after some weeks. Imogen didn't answer, but a few weeks later she said, "Your print's ready. Guard it. It's one of a kind."

Imogen had a very deep loyalty and respect for other people's feelings about her work, and she felt Martha wouldn't like that photograph. I think that over the years Imogen was hurt that Martha Graham never used any of her images. Martha is one of the most photographed people in this world, but most of the pictures you see of her are by Barbara Morgan. Imogen and I went to see Martha's group performing in 1974, I think,

in Berkeley, and we went backstage afterward. It was the first time they had seen each other in twenty years, and Martha's manager photographed the two of them together. The next year the group performed in San Francisco. We went again, and the young man took photographs again, and then he turned to Imogen and said, "I'll trade you." "I'm afraid I can't do that," Imogen said. "My work is now under a trust, and I'm not allowed to give pictures away." Afterward, when we came out of the theater, she said to me, "You know, that's not true about my not being able to give away pictures. I can do anything I darn please. But I wouldn't send him a picture of Martha Graham. You know how many I've taken of her, and she's never used them. She obviously doesn't like my photographs, so I couldn't possibly give one to him." It was very moving. All too few people have that kind of respect for another person's judgment.

Not only was Imogen totally devoted to her work; she expected that attitude of others too. She was very impatient with young people who wanted to call themselves photographers without the preparation it required. One day when I was there, about a year before she died, a young man called and offered to do anything at all for her, just to be around her. "Are you a cleaning man?" she said. "No, a photographer." "Well, how long have you been photographing?" "Six months," he said. "Then you keep working at it," Imogen said, "and call me back in ten years."

At one point, she had a print of that great Stieglitz, The Steerage, on the back of the couch where she used to put photographs for mulling over. I asked her why that particular image was there, and she said, "I'm sick and tired of these young people who claim they are photographers without knowing anything about other people's work. So when they come around, I ask them who did that. Here is a classic, and nine times out of ten they don't know. They are writing and photographing without having done their homework." Yet she gravitated to young people—she felt they could still learn. Imogen took the trouble to go to other people's shows, look at their work and react to it—particularly the work of young photographers. At the same time she tried to discourage a lot of them. I remember her asking one man what he liked to do besides photography. Work with his hands, he said. "Well, then," she said, "go be a plumber, you'll make a living." She discouraged those she didn't see something in, but it was also probably a way of letting them know it was hard work.

About a week before Imogen died, when she was feeling weak and helpless, I was helping her to get her photographic books in order so she could decide what distribution she wanted to make of them. Tom Eckstrom, her assistant, brought the mail up, and Imogen read aloud a letter from Burt Britton, who worked at the Strand bookshop in New York. He wrote that he'd been collecting self-portraits done by the artists and writers who came into the bookshop over the years, and he was going to publish them in book form. And to Imogen he said, "But how do I do it without the people whose work I love—you, for example: How do I do the book without you just because we've not met in the shop?" And he asked her for a self-portrait. Imogen said: "What I really ought to do is take a great big sheet of paper and on one side put a copy of that caricature Maynard Dixon did of me when I was pregnant with the twins, and then on the other side I'll draw a tiny, tiny circle, saying 'I've come to this.'" Then she took the letter and threw it on the discard file.

After she died I kept thinking about poor Burt Britton back in New York thinking he had had no response. So some months later I wrote him to tell him there had been a response, a great one, a graphic one.

FRED PADULA
Fred Padula, filmmaker

One day I was having lunch with Wynn Bullock and Imogen at her place, and one of them asked what film I was going to do next. We had been joking back and forth, and I said, "I guess I'll do one on the two of you." I hadn't really thought about it until that moment, but Wynn took me seriously, and I realized that it wasn't a bad idea. So that's how the film [*Two Photographers: Wynn Bullock and Imogen Cunningham*] began.

The film pretty much came out of two or three picnics when Wynn was up in San Francisco. Imogen would fix a lunch with her liver paté sandwiches and a lot of bananas—she was really into bananas—and we'd go out somewhere and I'd film them walking. Walking toward the camera, away from the camera, across the camera—they were both walkers. Then for the sound I taped them interviewing each other. A lot of it is gossip, a lot of it is kind of heavy stuff, and there are some interesting things when Imogen asks Wynn sincerely about his background and gets some pretty good answers. They were catalysts for each other.

Wynn had a very inquiring mind. He was continually questioning things; continually struggling to articulate his ideas; repeating himself to clarify his thinking, to make his complexities more relevant, less confusing. Imogen had a way of belittling all that. She felt that photography was a nonverbal thing. She did it naturally, and she didn't question or get caught up in words. At one point in the film the soundtrack picks them up on a panel at Foothill College. Someone in the audience had tried to connect Zen and photography—the sort of thing Imogen had no patience with. Of course Wynn saw no relationship between Zen and his work, but he tried to respond, and Imogen kept frustrating him. She said she had no idea what he was talking about, and it probably wasn't relevant, and it blended into all the other gobbledygook like Zen. She made the audience laugh at her wit at the expense of the serious ideas Wynn was trying to pursue. She got off on being witty. She capitalized on being witty, but much of the time her wit was at the expense of serious conversation.

Yet when she talked privately about Wynn's work, her sarcasm disappeared. She made fun of him as a philosopher, but she had tremendous admiration for him as a photographer. Not envy, just pure admiration and respect, probably more than she felt for any other photographer. She didn't talk about his work specifically, but then I don't recall her ever interpreting a picture. Her criticism would amount to saying a photograph was "student work" or "mature work." In the film someone asks about one of her photographs, and Wynn comments on it analytically, of course, but Imogen just says something like, "I was doing what came naturally." Which was true. She pointed the camera and let it happen. Sometimes she might direct something a little bit, but mostly what she did was to capture the essence of a situation. If it came out, fine. If it didn't, well, she had a lot of other photographs on the same roll. She didn't treat a negative preciously, or at least not until that particular negative had been reprinted and become important to her. She'd develop a roll of film and run off every frame, and if one was slightly out of focus she'd still use it if it has some quality of the person or the situation she liked. She made a photograph of me that was really out of focus. It looks as if she focussed on my ears rather than my nose. But that didn't bother Imogen. She printed up a bunch and gave them to my mother. And my mother likes them, and I like them. Imogen wasn't precious about such things.

When I was copying photographs for the film, she gave me a print of *The Unmade Bed* that had

Fred Padula JUDY DATER

a bunch of spots on it. I pointed them out to her, but she said, "It's just for a movie. If you want to touch it up, do it yourself." So I thought, okay, and I got all prepared to do it, and then I thought, "The hell with it. What am I doing touching up Imogen Cunningham's photograph?" So I copied it just as it was, and sure enough, you can see two or three little dust spots. I'm sure I'm the only one who notices them, but they're there, and I really admire her for being that casual.

Imogen could be very critical of people. She had no patience with people who didn't have good egos. She didn't like obnoxious people, but she really respected those, particularly young men, who had a realistically high regard for themselves. And another thing: she had a lot of contempt for old people. The first thing she'd comment on was their age and their ricketyness. Because, I think, she didn't see herself as old. In fact I don't remember her ever being with old people. She had older friends, but she always spoke of visiting them and keeping in touch as a duty. But young people she certainly related to, and she was in her glory with them.

I have a lot of fond memories of Imogen. We went camping several times, sleeping in my Volkswagen bus, and I remember waking up very, very early, about four-thirty or five in the morning, and looking out of the window. There would be Imogen, doing her exercises in the middle of the camping ground with the sun just rising. And I'd sleep for another hour or so and then about six o'clock she'd thump on the door and wake us up. She'd have a bowl of blackberries she'd picked in the fog, and we'd fix hotcakes with blackberry syrup and be on our way by six-thirty or seven. Not my idea of a normal hour to begin the day. And she was at least eighty-six then.

On one of those trips we stopped at a Safeway to pick up some groceries, and as I was driving the van out of the parking lot a man tried to pull into the lot in front of us and created a traffic jam—I couldn't back up and he wouldn't. He was shouting at me and calling me a hippie and being generally obnoxious. So Imogen reached into the sack of groceries and handed me a bunch of grapes, saying, "Here, give him these." His window was just below mine, so I just push-ed the grapes at him and he grabbed them automatically, not knowing what they were. He was so startled that he simply shut up and backed out in the direction he'd come from—didn't even try to get into the lot. And Imogen said, in a matter-of-fact way, "That's what he needed, some grapes."

Whenever we traveled Imogen would stop off and visit friends. There was hardly a town we'd come to where she didn't stop to pay a visit. The highlight of one trip in Oregon was the day we stopped to see Morris Graves. We drove up to an incredibly beautiful place in the middle of the redwoods, with a private lake and a wooden raft that floated out to a little island surrounded by lily pads. It was the most incredible setting, and just the kind of place you'd imagine Graves would live in. We drove through several gates, each with a big lock and a No Trespassing sign, and finally came to the house. Morris and Imogen greeted each other warmly, but very casually, as if they'd seen each other recently, although it had been a number of years. It was a warm, comradely sort of visit. He showed us his home and fixed us lunch, and told Imogen some of his recent experiences. How he had spent some time in India, and how he had smoked grass for the first time recently, suggesting that maybe these young people had something to offer the world. Imogen disapproved of that, but she didn't express it openly. Graves was an intuitive person. He wasn't wordy, his observations were casual, not too unlike Imogen's, and his conversation was on a personal level, not a philosophical one. Imogen really listened to him. She was very attentive, and the wit and sarcasm disappeared. She was quiet—not overly serious, but very relaxed, very peaceful with him. After a while I sensed they wanted to be alone. There was some kind of very intimate communion between them, something very strong and spiritual that I didn't fully understand. I was comfortable. I didn't feel left out, but I didn't feel part of it either. So I excused myself and went for a walk, exploring Morris Graves's environment.

While I was gone Imogen photographed Graves. I spent a couple of hours walking in the garden, rowing on the lake, and I had my own little spiritual experience. I'll never forget the house and the ferns and the redwood trees, and the lake with the lily pads. It was one of those places you can only experience once in your life, and you can never find it again. To go back would destroy the experience. I can't even remember how long we were there, but it affected me deeply, and it certainly affected Imogen, yet it was something we couldn't talk about. She retained that peacefulness long after, and it wasn't until the next day that her tongue took on the old knife-edge. It was as if she had had a union, a reunion with something.

BLANCHE PASTORINO

Blanche Pastorino, owner of Blanche's, restaurant/art gallery in San Francisco

Imogen added a great dimension to my life. She took me under her wing, and we went to museum openings, and art gallery openings, and poetry readings, and I met wonderful people through her. One exciting night I was invited to a supper party for twelve with people like Ansel Adams.

Blanche Pastorino JUDY DATER

I would never have been there in a hundred years if it hadn't been for Imogen. She used to tell me things about people she had known. I never dreamed that I would ever talk to someone who had actually known Virginia Woolf or Gertrude Stein.

But the greatest part of my friendship with Imogen was that she made me feel we had a one-to-one relationship. While we were together, it was just the two of us. Sometimes we were like two schoolgirls. She'd call me up and ask me to go somewhere—to drive her—and then she'd say, "What shall I wear?" Of course she wore wonderful things. I remember the first time I met her. A mutual friend had brought her to my little art gallery–restaurant. That day she was wearing a dress with a front of batik, and she wore stockings of purple lace, and her little black Mary Janes, and her little trademark fez. It was an exciting outfit. She said someone had sent her the batik, but it wasn't enough for a dress, so she had designed that dress with the purple back and sleeves.

One time after an opening we were having dinner at a Japanese restaurant on Fillmore Street when a very beautiful woman stopped by the table and introduced herself as a former designer for Elizabeth Arden. She said she was making a film on fashion design and she'd like Imogen to be in it. "Absolutely not," said Imogen, "I make my own style." Of course that's just why they wanted her in the film.

She gave me small gifts from time to time, especially cuttings and little plants. The most exciting plant I have was given to me not directly by Imogen, but by her son Pad after she died. It's a cutting from a geranium from Virginia Woolf's garden. And that same day Pad brought me this little hat of hers. She had over a hundred hats, but this was my favorite, and I always tried to get her to wear it. It's a wonderful thing, and someday I'm going to put it under a glass bell.

She liked my restaurant and understood what it meant to me. One day when I stopped by her house I was feeling a bit down, and she asked me what was the matter. And I said, "Oh, those people came in." She knew what I meant— "those people" are certain types who walk into my little place: they don't look right, they don't look left, they don't see a painting, they don't see a flower. They just march in and say, "What have you got to eat?" I do have very good food, and Imogen was very interested in food, but we both felt that there were so many more important things in life. Imogen used to say, "If food is your only interest, then this is not the place."

With Lawrence Ferlinghetti,
1975 JANET FRIES

And that's it—it's not just a restaurant. It hasn't been terrifically successful financially, but it has brought me things money could never buy. It brought me Imogen, and Buckminster Fuller, and Lawrence Ferlinghetti, and Ruth Asawa, and so many wonderful people I would never otherwise have known.

Lawrence Ferlinghetti comes to the restaurant quite often. One day I told him how fond Imogen was of his work—I had given her a copy of *Back Roads to Far Places*, a book I love. That pleased him, and later he called and asked if Imogen and I would like to come to a poetry reading he was giving at Lone Mountain College. Of course we went, and Imogen was the belle of the ball. This picture of Lawrence and Imogen was taken that night, and Lawrence inscribed it for me. I could have been in it, but I stepped away. I wish I wouldn't do things like that, but I always step away.

ANN HERSHEY

Ann Hershey, feminist, filmmaker, and writer

I was planning to do a film on photography, and I thought Imogen would be marvelous to narrate it. I didn't know her at the time, but she agreed to do it and invited me over for lunch. After a couple of hours with her I realized that she wasn't at all like the Imogen in John Korty's film about her: a sweet little lady, curt and very cute. Instead, we were talking about politics and the trouble I was having getting equal salary with the men I was working with at Channel 5, things like that. So I decided to make a film about her. We started the next weekend, and I continued shooting her for over three years.

All of the footage from the first year is still in the basement. I didn't use any of it because she was telling me the same things she had told everyone else, she was still *performing*. I realized that if I was to make a film that was different from the other films about her, I would have to break through that—I had to get her to trust me. Finally, after the first year, we began to get down to business. There's one scene in which she says, "Why didn't they discover me years ago? I was just as good." Then I knew we were on our way; she had begun to reveal things to me.

Generally, she was very agreeable to work with. She never tried to tell me what to do, she was always willing to work, and she enjoyed it. And at the end of the day when we were pack-ing up, worn out, ready to go home to bed, she'd announce that she was going out to dinner in an hour.

I loved John Korty's film, but he missed something by not letting Imogen tell us who she was. I think she liked my film. She said that mine had more of her in it.

She revealed a lot to me, both in the film and when we were alone. She knew I cared about her, and that I would hold what she told me private. I think none of us will ever know what went on inside her mind, though. She was a very contra-dictory person. When I first met her, I suppose I expected—the way you do when you meet someone older—someone who was very wise about life and about herself. But meeting Imo-gen, you didn't get that sense, that feeling that she knew who she was. I had expected someone a little more at peace with herself. She seemed rather bitter, and I felt she was very puzzled about who she was. A lot of that might be attrib-uted to the fact that she didn't really begin to be famous until she was in her late eighties. Much of that charade—that performing quality, the cape and the hats—was a way to keep people away from her. The cape was like a symbol, a way of folding in on herself. She loved attention, but there were times when she would be ter-ribly sarcastic to people, brutally cruel in a very funny way. But there were times too when the sarcasm was completely absent, and she could be a joy to be around.

Probably she was trying to figure herself out. It was a big change in her life: to have lived so long and then suddenly to find people coming all over her. Sometimes she'd be very tense with people demanding her attention, and then she'd worry whether she'd done the right thing. And then there was the reverse—she'd accept every invitation, do whatever anybody wanted her to do. She'd answer the phone and be very kind and nice, and then she'd hang up and say, "What a nuisance!" Or she'd be entertaining someone, and when the person left she'd say, "What a bore!" She was uneasy. She didn't handle the attention in a genuine way.

Perhaps it was because suddenly people were demanding her time, and she knew she had very little time left. In the photographs of her when she was younger there is a very kind expression in her eyes that seems to be missing in the close-ups of the film. Now she had a bit more money and she was free to try things, but she worried about how much time she had left. Yet she gave away her time, she was afraid to take time for herself. I'd call her up and ask her if we could shoot that weekend because the equipment was

Ann Hershey JUDY DATER

available—and she'd always agree. But then I'd hear her talking to someone on the phone, saying she would have loved to do this or that that weekend, but she had to shoot with Ann. You never knew what she really wanted. Part of her enjoyed the activity and attention, part of her wanted to be at peace. Probably at this point she knew she was committed to the public role, and she had to continue to work until she died. She was driven.

There was that little game she'd play about Ansel Adams. She was very jealous of him, all the things that Ansel has accomplished—his teaching, his books. She'd say, "I'd never have time for anything like that." Well, of course you make the time for something like that. And she didn't make enough time for her own work in the later years.

I was thrilled when she started working on *After Ninety*. She was fooling around with Polaroid like a little kid who's found a real tape machine —something new, lots of fun. Then she got into the serious thing. I think that business of going into the nursing homes to photograph was a way of working through her fear of going into a home. She was terrified of that, so she went in there and came out more determined than ever not to do it. More power in herself than ever.

She was shy, vulnerable to what people thought about her, and at the same time she could smash someone against the wall with one little witticism. She did it to me a couple of times. I used to wear a feminist symbol around my neck, and one time some woman asked me what it was. Imogen said, "Oh, she wears that so she'll know what sex she is." That hurt me. She knew I was gay and had talked about this with me before . . . how a lot of her best friends were women, but she didn't think she could love a woman. Still, she wasn't too comfortable, so that was a way of getting back at me for making her uncomfortable.

Sometimes when she was very tired there would be a slight glimpse of vulnerability. Certainly she came of a time when people weren't given to self-analysis or to sharing feelings the way our generation does. Imogen considered her feelings to be very, very private. In the film I worked so hard, so hard, to break through that.

Those conversations about marriage and women working—it was like pulling teeth. She just did not want to talk about it. There was no way she would talk about her divorce.

While we were working, she got down to business the moment I walked in the door. There was never any real interest in me personally, maybe because she did not want to have any kind of intimacy with me, or with any of us. There's no doubt she cared about me—she did very generous little things for me—but she was incapable of giving of herself. She did it in the photographs, she gave herself professionally, her time, her energy, her performance, but not what was deep down inside, not the pain.

In the film she says she's not a kissy person. We had never had any actual physical contact until right after she saw the film the first time. We were walking across the street and she took my arm. That was amazing. It told me that she liked the film and that she trusted me. That meant a lot, because I was terrified that day. We had invited a few people to the screening at the museum, and Imogen sat there watching with her face covered, and after it was over, she sat back there without saying a word. She didn't know what to think. Then Bill Heick leaned over and said he thought it was really good— she needed to hear that. Later, when we had gotten some awards, she began to realize that it was a good film and that maybe she was okay in it. That was such a personal thing, how she was coming across. She kept remarking that there were too many close-ups. And you know, it must have been very difficult, very hard combating someone like me; someone demanding to know how she felt about something when she didn't want to tell. She had a lot of guts.

Imogen loved life, really taught me a lot about living in the moment. Maybe that's the outcome of not being more intimate with people. You're not sitting around thinking about your problems or dwelling about the past. Maybe not sharing herself made it possible for her to continue being the active person she was.

She never wanted to analyze her work. And I think that's connected with not wanting to analyze herself. For the film I'd ask if she wanted to talk over a photograph, but no, she'd say it was fine. "They will see in it what they want to see, they will find out for themselves." And she said that also about herself. She said she was never going to write an autobiography, "They will find out for themselves." Maybe that's connected with the Victorian concept that you do not tell people who you really are inside, and you do not complain about your feelings, make people feel sorry for you. Perhaps she thought if she let us see her feelings she would begin to think about them and begin to feel sorry for herself, and she wouldn't allow that.

I was amazed that all of this time—here she was in her nineties—she had made no preparations for dying. I mean mental preparations, not practical ones. It would seem to me that you would start to close a few doors, you would start to do only the things you really wanted to do. Perhaps one of the reasons she seemed uneasy in herself at the end of her life was that she didn't want to die, she kept fighting it, she kept putting it off. Despite the vertigo, she wouldn't rest when she should. Of course, there are other ways to look at that. One might say she tried to ignore the vertigo because it meant she wouldn't be able to do more work. But it seems to me the responsibilities of life include dying. She certainly talked about it—she was very curious about the whole procedure. We talked about studies being made about the soul leaving the body, things

like that. But she didn't try to prepare herself to go out of life. She seemed to make it harder for herself.

The last bit of filming was the ceremony in Seattle, when Imogen received an honorary degree from the University of Washington. She asked me if I wanted to film it, and somehow I raised the money and drove up. A couple of days before we left, she phoned to say she had something for me . . . not money, but like money. The next day I got a letter with three twenty-dollar traveler's checks and a note: "Dear Ann, You know I don't want to contribute to anything to do with me, but why don't you use this for taxi fare?"

This was in 1974. She loved it—saw all her old friends, went to Mount Rainier where she had made the nude photographs. She was sparkling, and this time I think she really loved all the people because they were genuinely old friends, and she *did* want to spend time with them. She got us passes to the graduation hall, and giant yellow armbands. "Now they'll know you belong to me," she said. She kept looking around for us. At one point we were high up on a scaffold, and she looked up and waved and knocked her hat off. That final scene was just what we needed to give a little punctuation point. The whole thing was a great thrill for her, and it was just perfect.

Beaumont Newhall JUDY DATER

CHAPTER VI

Historians, Curators, Dealers

BEAUMONT NEWHALL

Beaumont Newhall, photography historian, photographer, former director of the International Museum of Photography at George Eastman House

She was a remarkable woman, of that there is no question. The period in photography Imogen covered is really fantastic. To think that she began in the days of the Photo-Secession and was photographing right up to 1976! There's something interesting that most people who have written about her haven't paid much attention: she was trained in Germany by one of the top photographic scientists, Dr. Robert Luther. There's a curious parallel there with Alfred Stieglitz's having studied with the top photographic scientist of the 1880s, Dr. Hermann Wilhelm Vogel. So she had very solid training, and I wish I'd talked to her about that. I did talk to her about platinum printing. She was a master of that, but she dropped it when the paper became difficult to get.

We also talked about Group *f*/64. She was one of the founding members, although I believe it was more the idea of Willard Van Dyke and Ansel Adams. The group had a very short, rather brilliant life, and I think we tend to exaggerate its importance because it was so spectacular for a while. Also, it's hardly possible to understand *f*/64 without knowing the low level of west coast photography in the 1930s. It was all Photo-Secession derivative, and there was William Mortensen, a very colorful Hollywood makeup artist, who shocked people with his subjects and who manipulated his photographs in a way that was considered an absolute no-no. Group *f*/64 was very, very doctrinaire. Imogen wasn't very excited about that; she just went along with it, without putting that passion into it that Ansel and Willard did.

One time when I was working on a reconstruc-tion of the enormous exhibition held in Stutt-gart by the Deutsche Werkbund in 1929, Imogen and I talked especially about the period of the late twenties and thirties. Imogen's pictures were in that exhibition, particularly the *Blumenformen* — she still used the German title for the flower forms. There was also a picture by Roger Sturte-vant, and she told me, incidentally, with the greatest of scorn, how now, when he was only in his *seventies*, he had worked out a darkroom in which he could do everything sitting down. Ri-diculous, she thought! And Roger reminded her of a story about Dorothea Lange. One day Dor-othea looked out of her studio window and saw a bread line. She had no film in her Graflex and she couldn't spare a minute, so she rushed up-stairs to Sturtevant's studio and asked to borrow a loaded magazine, and rushed out to take the picture. She came back, developed the negatives, and returned the magazine to Sturtevant. Roger said, "Are you sure you took all the septums out, Dorothea?" Oh yes, she was certain. But Sturtevant wasn't, and sure enough there was one she hadn't taken out, which he developed, and that's the famous picture.

Imogen loved to recollect, and she was very impressed by the pictures in the Stuttgart exhibi-tion. There were also a few pictures by Imogen in Dorothea Lange's collection that may or may not have been done about the time of the Stutt-gart show, but their imagery is German oriented. One is the Shredded Wheat tower; we look at it from beneath so that it appears to be a dark ob-ject with legs sticking out — a kind of space cap-sule effect. And there's the picture of the snake, a negative — about the only American picture

I've seen which uses the negative as an end in itself.

I admire the plant forms. I always thought they were very fine and I acquired quite a number for the collection at George Eastman House. And Imogen has done beautiful portraits. Her pictures of old people have an extraordinary character to them, like the one of her father by the woodshed. And that wonderful portrait with nobody there, the bed with the hairpins.

Her picture of Morris Graves is a great master-piece, in fact. It's an environmental picture, and I think that's characteristic of most of her best pictures. Like the one of the poet Theodore Roethke in 1959, against a great rock with a letter scratched and painted onto it. The Roethke and the Graves both have rather small figures in very large settings, yet in spite of that I don't feel the need for a close-up. In the Morris Graves there is a tenderness and a very sensuous appreciation of his features.

That picture of Stieglitz was made in 1934—

Shreaded Wheat Tower, 1928
IMOGEN CUNNINGHAM

92

he would have been seventy then. It was about that time I met him, and he was a pretty crotchety character. He wasn't interested a bit in having his picture taken or really in talking much about photography. Imogen told me how she went to him and insisted on taking his portrait and finally broke him down. She had to borrow his old camera, which he hadn't used for some time, and they spent an hour putting it up—they had to tie it together. But it's a very fine picture of Stieglitz.

There's one thing I've always admired about Imogen: she never followed any particular trend, never allowed herself to be captured. There was a joint interview in *U.S. Camera* [1955] with Imogen, Ansel, and Dorothea, in which she effectively put down the whole idea of documentaries, which had been passionately described by Dorothea. Imogen made some remarks about the danger of getting into a trap, thinking in a circle, and she wanted to be free of that.

Her double exposures are very interesting. Whether or not they were accidents or made deliberately doesn't matter to me. There's so much talk of previsualization, but the important thing is not previsualization but recognition. One special thing about photography is that there is a great deal recorded on the film that the photographer never sees at the time he is making the photograph. That's a great difference between a drawing and a photograph. An artist can draw only what he sees or imagines; the photographer can capture something accidentally, and recognition becomes the important thing. Imogen had that ability.

Determination and persistence were absolutely characteristic of her. Imogen really went after things in a very fine way. In that she was typical of the earlier women photographers. In fact, she fits very neatly into the whole pattern of women photographers of her period, that group that began in Photo-Secession: Gertrude Käsebier, who was second only to Steichen as far as Stieglitz was concerned; Jessie Tarbox Beals; Frances Benjamin Johnston; Annie Brigman; even Dorothea Lange began as something of a Photo-Secession type. There's no question that a large number of women were attracted to photography in the early part of the twentieth century.

I've never seen a different sensibility in women photographers, but those women had one thing in common—drive. They had resistance and drive and energy. You can go right back to Mrs. William Henry Fox Talbot. It's not generally known that she was one of the first photographers. She learned from her husband and was his printer. The most forceful nineteenth-century photographer of either sex was Julia Margaret Cameron. She bullied people in front of the camera. Gertrude Käsebier was a very strong individual. Obviously, Dorothea Lange couldn't have been that kind of documentary photographer without being persistent, and Margaret Bourke-White had a drive that was unbelievable. Laura Gilpin is another like that—in her eighties, insisting that the pilot strap her in and take out the door of the plane when she's flying over the Canyon de Chelly.

I don't know if that kind of drive was unique to the women photographers, but it was certainly characteristic—and Imogen certainly had it.

It's somewhat difficult to judge Imogen's position in the stream of photographic history. Her personality was so extraordinary, her enthusiasm so great, and she maintained so many friendships, that I think her personality may color my thinking about her work. She was tired of hearing about her plant forms of the 1920s, but they were a really fine contribution. She brought a very original point of view to that particular field. And after that period, her pictures of people and portraits are her most important work, particularly portraits of artists and people close to her. The environmental portrait is her strongest area, and some of her portraits without anybody present are very witty. I certainly think that she will be remembered. She's one of the very few American photographers who have had international recognition during their lifetime.

ANITA VENTURA MOZLEY

Anita Ventura Mozley, photography historian, curator of photography at Stanford University Museum of Art

There are a number of things I always meant to ask Imogen, but somehow I never did. Her sense of the relationship between the impetus to write and the impetus to make photographs, for instance. I meant to ask her about the kind of writing that influenced her. She was very much interested in the literature of the turn of the century or a little earlier, writers like William Morris and fantasies like his *The Wood beyond the World*, and she used it in a way no other photographer did. She used the camera to illustrate, and that seemed to be a very unusual impulse. The dress-up was part of that too. She achieved a very strange feeling in some of those early photographs. The portrait of John Butler, for instance, the platinum print. He is wearing a bracelet and has a kind of batik draped over his shoulder and is sitting in front of a painting that looks like a Gustav Klimt. A marvelous photograph. When I first saw it there was something written underneath it, something like "King Solomon," but after I got the photograph—I bought it for the museum—I saw she had erased that, and it was now "Portrait of John Butler." But even without that other title there's evidence of an impulse to create another world.

She attached a great importance to the derivation and exact meaning of words. When she mentioned Lillian Hellman's *Pentimento* to me—she often recommended books to me—she commented that she wondered if Hellman had ever seen her photograph of Morris Graves with that title and shared her interest in the meaning of the word.

In any case, Imogen was very well read and had looked at a lot of art, and these things combined to make her the kind of artist in photography she was. She saw things and she *recognized* them, which I think is the essential act of the photographer, to recognize things at many levels. Until the *After Ninety* book she never had a continuous story to tell. In photographs she just set things up so that they had many different levels of meaning. It's somewhat related to different levels of meaning in good poetry.

There is something of that in the Morris Graves portraits and in the *Phoenix Recumbent*. The plant forms are different, more abstract. They are very, very beautiful—masterworks—related to certain kinds of painting, like Georgia O'Keeffe's. They came out of a period when knowledge of the art of the early twentieth century was being used quite a bit in photography, and they are related more to painting than to photography at its purest—that is, the immediate transcription of some recognition the photographer has picked out of the world. The plant forms are posed in the way studio portraits are. There's a playing with light and shapes, like exercises in a kind of light abstraction—they might have been done with paper cutouts. They are probably the best things of that sort that had ever been done, but to me they are not essentially photographic. An article about the *Tower of Jewels* [the close-up of the magnolia calyx] appeared in *Architectual Review* in the early thirties, and it's interesting that they should have been published there rather than in an art journal. The *Tower of Jewels*, just because of the quality of the plant itself, is different. It's much less linear, the gradations of tone are softer, it's not so abstract. It's more like the photographs that seem to seize something about the subject on different levels.

Some of Imogen's portraits have that multi-level quality. The portraits of Roi Partridge, especially the one of him with the etching press, and another in front of one of his etchings—the best portraits of him that could have been taken. Certainly the ones of Edward Weston and Margrethe Mather—that whole series seems to talk about that relationship and Weston's dandyism. There are ones in which they are posed separately and they look sort of like Bonnie and Clyde. And there is the one in a rather dark room, with Margrethe bringing out rolls of paper on one side and Edward at the other. There's a kind of romanticism to it, but it's more taking a normal working situation—Margrethe was actually bringing paper out of the darkroom—and using it to tell about the relationship between Margrethe and Weston.

The first time I met Imogen on a more than casual basis was in 1972, when I went to her house with my husband to buy three photographs of Mather and Weston for the museum. We talked for a long, long while — or rather, Imogen talked to Robert. The way things had gone for her in her youth must have made her find men much more interesting to talk to than women. Anyway, she did rather drop me for Robert that afternoon, and he enjoyed it immensely. The phone was ringing constantly, and finally three young men showed up to take her to a show and then dinner. Imogen led a very lively life. As my first introduction to her it was amazing.

I loved to hear her voice on the phone or in person. It seemed to me one of the most glamorous voices I'd ever heard. There was a softness to it, and the things she said were so sharp — always a little conflict between the two elements. There was an essential sweetness to Imogen, though. No matter what sharp thing she said, there was a justness, and underneath a kind of sweet understanding of how strange and erratic people are.

Anita Mozley JUDY DATER

Sometimes when she was being thorny she was sticking up for ideas about photography she believed in. I think she never wanted photography to be a terrifically big deal. It seems to me that when any kind of art is subjected to a great pitch of publicity you can hardly see it anymore. It becomes invisible, the way a national monument becomes invisible. And of all the arts photography can't be treated that way. You have to be close, be intimate with it. So when Imogen made tough remarks about people who were really *operating* in the world of photography, I think she was fighting for a kind of independence —she never wanted to be part of any group. I read an interview with Imogen that appeared in some journal in Seattle around 1914. It was interesting that so many things she said then she was still saying up to the time of her death. She determined very early who she was and what she was doing, and her belief in independence, the value of practical work and experience, the honesty of response—all that was formed very early on.

One of the things I loved about Imogen was her devotion to the real world, to every observable thing. When we were talking I noticed her eyes measuring things. Her eyes were always so hungry—really *looking*. She got a thrill in seeing any kind of new thing, or even in seeing some old thing in a new form. She was a person of intense recognitions, and I think that's why she was a great photographer.

MARGERY MANN

Margery Mann, photography historian, critic, writer, photographer

In the early sixties I was working for *Artforum*, and I called Imogen for some press prints for reviewing the show she was having at the San Francisco Museum. She invited me to lunch and we found we had a lot in common—gardening, for instance —and we took it from there and became good friends. In 1973, when the University of Washington Press approached her to do her second book, Imogen asked me to do the text, and miraculously, we remained good friends afterward.

In a way it was very difficult working with her because fairly often we'd disagree on prints. There were some I'd keep rejecting and putting back in the stack, and she'd keep pulling them out again. There was a photograph called *The Box*, a girl looking through a box in Monterey, which I kept putting on the bottom of the pile; Imogen thought it was wonderful and kept pulling it out. But I was the one who was putting the prints in the book, so in the end I usually won when we disagreed.

I saw Imogen as a hard-core romantic who tried not to be. Even her realism was actually extremely romantic. She started with those very pictorial things inspired by William Morris, and that attitude never really left her. The techniques became more classical, but there is still a romantic feeling in some of her later work which is really remarkably similar to the pictorialists. Some of her photographs of Phoenix—*Dream Walking*, for instance—are pictorialism in its essence. Imogen tried very hard to be a purist, I always felt, but she just didn't have it in her. That last photograph of Morris Graves in his leek garden is very romantic. And so is the Man Ray image. "Just the pure print," she'd say, but she had a double standard. It was all right for Imogen to play in the darkroom, but it wasn't so good if anybody else did. Now Weston *was* a purist; he worked strictly to the 8 x 10 format. Imogen never worried about format; she cropped the hell out of anything she wanted to. Imogen talked purist and did just what she pleased.

She tried sometimes to be a documentarian, but I don't think she was. Perhaps she was trying to prove she was an all-round photographer. She talked once about doing a book of her documentary photographs of San Francisco and showed me a lot of things, but they didn't go very deep. I think her best documentary is the *Coffee Gallery*, but that's really a portrait.

Imogen has undoubtedly been an important influence in west coast photography. She was one of the *creative* people in the *f*/64 group. There was Edward Weston and Ansel Adams and Imogen, and the rest of the group were followers. These three had ideas and carried them out, and they were influential in changing the course of west coast photography from pure pictorialism

to pure seeing. Or what they thought was pure seeing—I think Weston was a romantic too. But in any case, the *f*/64 exhibition in 1932 was a revolutionary exhibition, and the *f*/64 movement became a dominating, and in some ways an inhibiting force in California photography. There were too many little Edward Westons for a very long time.

Imogen was willing to try anything, and I think her experimental approach was influential. An awful lot of people have looked at things differently because Imogen saw them in a certain way. Plant forms, for example, and her studies of people in their environments. Imogen was influ-

Margery Mann JUDY DATER

ential through that experimental attitude, rather than in terms of the pure vision she espoused.

Weston influenced Imogen very much in the early twenties, but then he went his way and she went hers. The contact between them was lost for a while when Weston went off to Mexico, and it was at that time that Imogen began to do that formal examination of objects. She was stuck at home with the kids, so she was doing plant forms; Weston was examining palm trees in Mexico, and Strand was examining machinery, and Renger-Patzch was examining things in Germany. It was a time when a great deal of formal examination was being done, and I think these people were working independently. I think Imogen didn't know what Weston was doing in Mexico.

There was a period in her life when Imogen didn't photograph much. There wasn't much work between 1915 and the twenties, when the kids were small and she was simply stuck on the Mills College campus. She did an awful lot of portraits of Mills College girls and they were dreadful—just hack work. I kept trying to get her to throw them out, but she wouldn't. She told me that she had been terribly frustrated by not being able to work then, and I think she turned to photographing plants essentially because she couldn't get out to photograph people. I suspect she didn't think those plant photographs were particularly important until they were accepted for that prestigious Deutsche Werkbund show. That gave her a different perspective on them, and that kind of feedback was important to her in evaluating her own work.

With Weegee, about 1946 KENNETH HOWE

The *Magnolia Blossom* was done at that time. About 1925, I think. But Imogen dated things very casually. She was always very positive, except that one day she'd give one date for a photograph, and another day another date. People loved her *Magnolia Blossom*, but she got so she hated it. She printed and sold more of that photograph than any other, and she got sick of being identified by it. Dorothea Lange once told her that she would be remembered for her plant photographs, and Imogen said, "But I have photographed everything that can be exposed to light."

She was never analytical about her own work. She felt that it was visual and should be accepted by the person looking at it. Part of that was a reaction to Minor White and his over-verbalization. She was very scornful about verbalization, and very scornful about how academic photography was becoming. The photography scene was now being controlled by the people in the schools rather than by the photographers, and she found that unhealthy.

She did talk about other photographers' work, but she didn't speak highly of many people. Strand was her favorite because he was so classical. His work was classical in the *f*/64 tradition, according to her theories. He did things the way that they should be done, whether she did or not. She didn't like the work of a good many other photographers because she felt that they were polluting the medium in a way. Arbus, for instance.

One day she ran into Arbus on McAllister Street, and afterward she said to me, "You know, Margery, she was terribly nasty to me"— and I wondered why she would be nasty to this nice little old lady. "All I did was ask her why she photographed all those freaks and things." I guess Arbus bristled.

As far as I know, Imogen never had a student, a private student. She preferred to teach in a more structured situation, although she was scornful of the schools that were attracting all those photography students. She felt that most students were expecting to have a little hole drilled into their heads and knowledge would be poured into it, and that they'd be much better off studying on their own. They'd learn more, and they'd learn more deeply. But Imogen was willing to teach, and she taught a great number of workshops. Of course, there was a lot of ham in Imogen, and she liked to have large situations to project it in.

She liked putting on an act—the Imogen act. I always wondered when she began costuming herself as Imogen. The earlier photographs show her as dowdy, kind of frumpish, and I wonder when she began to use the cape and the mirrored hat. Anyway, someplace along the line she began to develop the character of Imogen professionally. Perhaps it was when she felt she was old enough not to have to conform—like the line from Eliot's *Love Song of J. Alfred Prufrock*: "I grow old, I grow old, I shall wear the bottoms of my trousers rolled."

Of course, her old age and the explosion of interest in photography coincided. The interest in photography was largely responsible for the first book on Imogen in 1970. It was terribly important to her, a culmination of her life. There she was, in her late eighties, and the book brought her attention that she had never had before, and I think that pushed her a bit more toward image creation. She became a legend as a very old person who was still working, still creative, and so it also became important to her to keep that image going. I think that was the reason for the *After Ninety* book.

What she found in doing *After Ninety* was terribly discouraging to her. So many of the people were just vegetables. She wanted to photograph only those who had some spark, but every so often she'd get suckered into photographing a person who was no longer alert. Even in the last year, when she felt so rotten so much of the time, she kept up her act and pushed herself as hard as she could, as long as she could. People, relative strangers, would come over to see her— Imogen had as many visitors as the Golden Gate Bridge—and they'd try to leave after a decent time, but she'd grab onto them like the ancient mariner, and they'd stay another couple of hours. And afterward Imogen would complain bitterly about it, but much of it was her own fault. I think she did it because she wanted to keep being part of the world as long as she could. I think she was lonely, living in that house by herself, and holding people a little longer was a way of avoiding loneliness, a way of saying, I am ninety-some years old and people still seek me out. It was very important to her that photographers like Arnold Newman and Brassaï would come to see her. She used her energy to make herself worth seeking out and to keep contact with people, because people really turned her on.

HELEN JOHNSTON

Helen Johnston, director of Focus Gallery, San Francisco

In August of 1966 I was thinking about opening a photography gallery, and I'd been looking for a good location. Finally I found something on Union Street, a perfectly dreadful looking place, with plaster falling, and pink and green walls. I knew I could take care of the plaster and the paint, but what concerned me was the fact that it was up two flights. Still, the place was ideal in every other way and all I could afford, so I decided to ask for someone's opinion. I had never met Imogen, and naturally she had never heard of me, but I phoned her cold turkey, told her my plans and that I was very much concerned that people wouldn't be interested enough to walk up those two flights. Imogen answered quick as a flash, "It wouldn't bother me, and if it wouldn't bother me, it shouldn't bother anybody else." And it didn't bother her. She continued coming to the gallery for the rest of her life, whether the show was important or not.

She was more supportive than almost anyone else in the early years. I had asked a number of prominent photographers if they would like to have the opening show, but they had never heard of me and didn't want to take the risk. I hadn't even asked Imogen, but she was always supportive anyway. Of course, I showed her work later—in fact, twice. She's the only one I've ever repeated; there's so much being done in photography that it's my policy not to repeat.

I watched Imogen grow as a living legend through those ten years. When she first came to the gallery, people would go up and talk to her in a casual, friendly way, but gradually more and more awe crept in. In the last three years of her life, the visitors would come to me and say in hushed tones. "Is that Imogen Cunningham?" I'd urge them to go up and say hello, but often they'd be hesitant. Toward the end they wanted to photograph her. The last time she came several people asked, so she sat in a chair with her back to the window, turning her head this way and that, and then she looked at one of them and said in that quick, birdlike voice of hers, "Well, how many more hundreds of photographs do you want to take of me?" That closed the session.

Imogen expressed her opinions about what was on exhibition—very strong opinions—though usually not to me. She would talk to someone else viewing the pictures, then others would join the group, and very soon there was a conducted tour of the show, with Imogen as a guide, expressing her opinions as fact. Not "I think," or "in my opinion," but as fact. I could see that the group accepted her words that way, and that wasn't good, but it was interesting to see the effect she had on an audience.

Whether a print was a vintage print or contemporary, whether she had printed it herself or someone else had done it—those questions were completely irrelevant to Imogen. She felt the idea of a vintage print represented a set of false values; it was an artificial standard that annoyed her very much. When the Trust started making prints I'd never ask her if a print had been made by the Trust or by her, because it was like waving a red flag in front of a bull. The whole idea of the Trust was to perpetuate her work in terms of the strength of the image and the quality of the print—those were the things that mattered.

There was one memorable incident that showed me just how strongly she felt about that. An antique dealer and his wife who were in San Francisco for a few days brought in a picture that they had purchased in New York as an early Imogen Cunningham. But it had no authentication, no signature, and they wanted to know if I could get some verification. I agreed to show it to Imogen when I went over to her house the next morning. As they were about to leave town, I told them to ring me from the airport to find out what she had said, and then I would mail the print back. So the next morning I showed the print to her and she looked at it silently for quite a while. Suddenly, before I could possibly have stopped her, she tore it to bits. I was stunned. After a long moment I said, "But Imogen, that print didn't belong to me. I was entrusted with it just to ask you if it was yours." "Yes," she said, "I did it, but it was a terrible print. I don't want it around. Don't worry, I'll see those people get a better print."

There was nothing to do. Shaking in my boots, I answered the phone when the man called from the airport. "I've got wonderful news for you," I said. "Not only is the print by Cunningham, but she wants you to have a better print." "That's great," he said, "I am lucky"—and never once mentioned having the vintage print returned.

Imogen called later and apologized, and it worked out all right, but the story illustrates perfectly how Imogen felt about prints and about what she thought were false values based on when a print was made and who made it.

No matter what your age, Imogen was above all a now person. When Laura Gilpin, who was then about eighty-five, had her show here, Imogen invited the two of us to dinner at her favorite Vietnamese restaurant. I thought it would certainly be an interesting evening, because surely they would reminisce about the old days in photography and those great people they knew. But the conversation was entirely in the present. Those two women talked about their TV commitments, and their book commitments, and what they were doing at that moment. I was disappointed in a way, but it was pretty impressive to see how completely they were living in the present.

LEE D. WITKIN

Lee D. Witkin, director of The Witkin Gallery, Inc., New York City

When I opened the gallery I didn't know that much about the people working in photography, and I might very well not have heard of Imogen at that time. A few months later, in July 1969, I was in San Francisco, basically to meet with Cole Weston about his father's work, and someone said I should call up Imogen. I did, and she invited me to her house at 1331 Green Street. She was very nice, unpretentious, friendly, very inquisitive about my gallery and what I was doing. Not old at all. She was *herself*—I think you reach a stage in life when you have become what you are and age no longer makes any difference.

She treated everybody the same, whether young or old. She really was very young because she was interested in what was happening, she always wanted to know the latest gossip, and she was a mine of information about everybody else. She'd gossip about everybody, and she was able to bring past and present together.

I started to handle her work at thirty-five dollars a print, and in the beginning she would ship me things by UPS. The packages had to be exactly weighed, but she didn't have a scale in her house, so she would take them down the hill to a butcher shop, weigh them, and trudge back up the hill and pack them for UPS. She was marvelous to work with. I'd write her for a print and about a week later it would arrive. Other photographers take anywhere from a month to five years.

She was fun, and she *wanted* to be fun. She wanted to be unpredictable. She enjoyed the role of old lady because she could say anything and get away with it. She loved to deflate egos. Imogen was also something of a vamp—she loved men. Whenever I was in southern California I made a point of flying up to San Francisco to see her. The most wonderful time I ever spent with her was the year before she died. I was in

LA with Howard Daitz, and I urged him to fly up with me for the day. So Imogen had three beaux all to herself—Howard, Tom Eckstrom, and me—and she was in her glory. She was so girlish, putzing around and preparing food and serving us. It was incredible to see that girlish part of Imogen. Another time I called her and mentioned that Betty Hahn, the photographer, was with me. She didn't like that. She didn't like the idea of my coming cover to see her with a girl. She told me about Willard Van Dyke. "Willard always calls me when he comes to California," she said. "He always comes to see me, and he always takes me out to dinner—

Lee D. Witkin JUDY DATER

alone." "Okay, Imogen," I said, "next time I come, I'll take you out, *alone.*"

She was marvelous company. In fact, she never stopped talking. And her little house was incredible—always in disarray, yet she managed to type letters and make prints. Most of the years I knew her she did everything herself: printing, drymounting, billing. Sometimes the prints would be crooked on the mount and poorly spotted, and a customer would mention it. But I'd say, "You're kidding. Imogen was ninety when she made this print. Do you think I'm going to tell her she didn't spot it and it's a little crooked? You take it the way it is." Of course at seventy-five dollars, which is what her prints were for most of the time I represented her, they seem like the buy of the century. And I remember that for her first show we raised them from thirty-five to fifty dollars.

That was in 1972, I think. She was leery of charging even fifty dollars. In a way she had a tremendous sense of inferiority, because she never did sell prints until the very end, and even her portrait sittings were incredibly underpriced. She did not have a big ego. She knew she was good, but she was never confident that people would pay a lot of money for her work—except for the platinum prints. She insisted they should go to a museum and I used to get down on my knees and beg her to sell me platinum prints. And then on most occasions I had to promise her I would keep them in my own collection—and I was honored.

Her prints didn't really begin to sell until three or four years ago; most photographers weren't able to sell well until recently, anyway. Also, in the early seventies Imogen was still making prints, and I find that collectors are very reluctant to buy work that's readily accessible—they'd rather jump in when someone's dead. Look at Arbus. I had Arbus prints no one would buy, but as soon as she died they wanted them, at any price. That was the situation with Imogen. It changed only in the last two years of her life, when she became a celebrity through interviews and exposure. The two books on her, the show she had—they really launched her. Before that she was just a nice old lady who took photographs.

I have a really strong opinion about Imogen's photography. I think she is much, much better than anyone gives her credit for. I remember being furious with Gene Thornton when he reviewed her show for *The New York Times*. It covered from 1901 to 1972 or 1973: pictorialism, $f/64$, plant studies, portraits, and Haight-Ashbury hippies. His comment was that she had never worked in any main style, that all she had done was produce a lot of nice pictures! She did work in many styles, and she explored each one, and she changed, but that doesn't make her or her vision any less valid. Anyone who works in a medium for seventy-five years and doesn't change ends up repeating himself—like Chagall, who's been forging his own work for the last forty years. Imogen was always fresh. Unfortunately, some of the best work has never been published. I know several male nudes that I think are comparable to Weston's best, and there must be dozens of images of this quality that have not been published. As with any major artist, a lot of mediocre work has been selected along with her good work, so you get a diluted impression of her strength. When she was good, which was much of the time, she was absolutely first rate. A really good editing of her work would put her in the first rank of photographers.

When I put her shows together I was more or less at her mercy. She would drag out two or three hundred things, and I would take a hundred. But I'm sure there were several hundred more she didn't show me from which I could have made a better show. She didn't even realize herself what she had. The photograph of the two calla lilies, for example. For five years she couldn't find the negative.

My favorite photograph is the male nude bending at the waist. She photographed a section of the torso so that it looks almost like a shell—absolutely fantastic. I think her plant forms, other male nudes, the unmade bed—these are the classics. And the magnolia flower—justifiably a classic; it's beautiful, so affirmative. I would say that her best work was done in the twenties, thirties, and forties. I don't much like the hippie portraits of the sixties. I do think the portrait of Morris Graves in the fifties is exceptional, and the later portrait of him in the seventies is equally fine.

She did ask me for my opinion. I think she considered me some kind of Merlin because I could sell her work, particularly in New York. We did very well by her, but I considered her a friend more than just a client. When we were together we hardly talked business at all. We talked about people and life, and so on. Of course, when she set up the Trust there were a lot of details to talk about. She had a lot of foresight. She was a woman of action and she did a very wise thing in setting up the Trust so that her work didn't become a heavy legacy for her children, didn't make a tax burden. All in all, she was a very capable woman. I think that was one of the reasons she left her husband. She said he treated her as if all she could do was the dishes.

I suppose I was really so wrapped up in the friendship with Imogen that the business relationship was almost secondary. She would give me little presents—books and jam. The last time it was orange marmalade. Back in New York I noticed that the label said "Imogen's Orange Marmalade, Type 2." Next time I saw her I asked her what Type 1 was. "Oh," she said, "Type 1 was a disaster." I used to send her hats, as did other friends. I wanted to send her things for her birthday, but there really wasn't much you could get her. When she was ninety-one I mentioned that Gene Smith had said to tell her that ninety-one was just nineteen backwards. She got a big kick out of that. And for her ninety-second birthday I sent her a yellow canvas director's chair with *Imogen* on the back. She kept it in her living room, and I noticed that the chair was there at her memorial service in the park.

I think Imogen sometimes thought up lines and saved them. And if they got a laugh, she'd use them again. She really played to an audience, but in the nicest way.

She didn't do that in her photographs, though.

Imogen and Lee Witkin as Margrethe Mather and Edward Weston, 1974–1975   LINDA CONNOR

They were really a one-to-one relationship with herself. You have to separate the photographs from the person. There was an artist involved only with herself in the photographs, and there was a performer at work in her relationships with people.

I loved to get letters from her. They were very forthright and funny. She had a typewriter in her little workroom and she tossed them off, just the way she talked. I'm glad to know that she wrote to a lot of people, because that way she may have created something of an autobiography. I often urged her to write a book about her past. She was a walking history really, a history of the *whole* of California photography from the beginning of the century. She knew everybody. She worked with Weston, she visited August Sander, she knew Coburn—it's staggering. She could have left you breathless, but she was so direct, so much of the moment, that her accomplishments and the scope of her experience didn't dawn on you.

I especially admired the portrait she did of Margrethe Mather and Edward Weston—the one with Margrethe's head on Weston's shoulder. It's so romantic and so beautiful. I wanted to be photographed with Imogen like that, and one day I set up the shot and handed Linda Connor my camera to photograph it. Of course it doesn't look at all like Imogen's photograph, and I look terrible, but the shot is touching, and Imogen was marvelous; she held her hand so delicately, just the way Margrethe did. I think there are ugly-beautiful, beautiful-ugly people, and Imogen was one. It was amazing that given her physical appearance she could really be so beautiful. Beauty really is inside.

Arthur Shartsis JUDY DATER

106

CHAPTER VII

Business Matters

ARTHUR SHARTSIS, *part 1*

Arthur Shartsis, attorney, trustee of The Imogen Cunningham Trust

I was a lawyer for one of the big firms in San Francisco, and one day in 1974 someone in the probate department called me and said that an old lady named Cunningham had phoned, and did I know anything about her? I was the only one in the firm who took photographs, so he called me. It turned out not to be a probate matter at all. Imogen had been thoughtlessly referred to the probate department simply because of her age, but what she wanted was to establish a kind of trust.

The first meeting was really terrific. It was in this law firm conference room, a huge room with steel engravings of chief justices on the wall, gray hair and pinstripe suits all around — and there was Imogen. She told us that she'd gotten the Guggenheim award a few years before and things were going very well for her. Now she had all these prints and this money, and she wanted to know what to do with it. She didn't like museums. She felt that museum politics change, and after you die your work can be put on the back shelf and never be shown. We had a long discussion about her ideas, and at the end I said something about her being poor before, but now she was rolling in it. "Well," she said, "I wouldn't say I'm exactly rolling in it, but at least when I need a new bra I can buy one." Complete shock and consternation in the room.

That's how the whole thing started. Because of her concerns about museums, and because she wanted her descendants to benefit from the value of her work, she was interested in creating some kind of institution that would make money as well as retain the integrity of her work. That's a lot different from the thinking of most people, who usually look toward immortality only and don't concern themselves with an institution's supporting itself. But it was ingrained in her that she worked for profit, so those ideas pointed toward the Trust.

The Trust idea itself was new, and that interested her. I don't think there is another legal institution like it, especially in the arts. She needed an institution to retain the integrity of her work, to perpetuate it, market it, print it, and to have autonomy even when she was alive to do a lot of those things herself — that was absolutely unique. And she had the flexibility to accept something that new.

She also had the flexibility to accept advice. It only dawned on me a couple of years later that she had probably never worked with a corporate lawyer before. She was about ninety-one years old, and it was the first time she'd come to a downtown-type lawyer, but she adapted to it incredibly well. After a while she learned how to be a good client. If something had to be negotiated, she'd have me do the dirty work; if she had problems, she knew when to call; she knew what advice to follow and what not to follow. That's fairly unusual. It takes even quite sophisticated people a while to know when to call, and it never entered my mind that the whole thing was a new experience for her in her nineties.

The plan for the Trust was that we'd have three trustees — Adrian Wilson, Imogen's son Gryff, and myself — and we'd operate with Imogen present so we'd get in practice for the day she died. If she hadn't been willing to recognize that she was going to die, the Trust never could have worked. But for a year or more the four of us would sit around together and we'd say, "How do we do this?" And Imogen would say,

"I'd do it this way," and we'd do it that way. Occasionally the trustees would prevail. After a while the trustees began to make the decisions more independently, so when the Trust met a few days after Imogen died, we kept operating exactly as if she were there. That was possible only because she didn't cling while she was alive. She knew that the trustees were going to have to operate the Trust, and if they didn't have the chance to learn, it wouldn't work. It wasn't that she wasn't interested or didn't have the energy; it was that she had decided to do it that way— to give the trustees a free hand, but also to put them in a position to reflect her judgment. So she worked right along with us, shared in the judgments, but let us make the final decisions. That kind of detachment is unique.

One of the concerns of the Trust was to alleviate her work load. Imogen did everything herself— she answered her own phone, wrote her own letters, developed her own negatives—and it was only with a crowbar that we could pry her away from some of her chores. When the Trust was set up she was concerned, as we all were at first, whether it would make money. So she started moonlighting, doing portraits on the side to make a little money. The Trust in fact began to make a substantial income, certainly more than enough to support her and to pay everyone's costs, so I'd call her every month or so and ask if she needed any money. Taxes were coming up, did she need a new camera or anything, the money was just accumulating. But she always refused, and finally we learned that she was moonlighting. "Fine," I said, "if you want to do that, but you know it would save paperwork if we ran it through the mechanism we've set up."

And then there was the Rolleiflex. She had used an old Rollei for a long time—it was out of date, she couldn't see through the fresnel screen, it was dark—and she kept talking about replacing it with a rebuilt. And I'd urge her to get a new one, telling her she deserved good equipment and she could afford it. But nothing happened. Then one day I got a call from Imogen, who was in a camera store. "Hi. How much money do I have?" I asked her what she wanted to do. Buy a new camera. "Well," I said, "you certainly have enough money for that." And she said, "Do you know how much a new camera costs? Seven hundred and sixty dollars!" "That sounds all right." "It does?" "Yes, that sounds fine." But then she said, "Do you know how much the case for it costs? Sixty dollars! Do you think I can afford one of those?" I assured her she could, and she bought it on the spot. It was amazing. Part of it was knowing that she couldn't use the camera for long, and she didn't want to waste money that way.

DANEE MCFARR

Danee McFarr, administrator of The Imogen Cunningham Trust, formerly Imogen's archivist

I was working as a photo archivist at the Maritime Museum when one of the people the museum did business with asked me if I would like to catalogue Imogen Cunningham's negatives. So he had me call her up, and I went around the next day at nine-thirty. It was hardly a job interview. I was probably the only photo archivist anyone knew in the area, so I got the job. I stayed on part time at the museum and I started working at Imogen's two days a week in late January of 1975. Mainly the job was to catalogue the negatives so they would be easily accessible to anyone. Imogen had her own filing system and usually could retrieve a negative quickly, but it would have been impossible for anyone else. So I had to number all the negatives and develop a card file system with cross-references. And the other part of the job was to work with Imogen trying to fill in information that was missing from the negative envelopes, try to find dates. On lots of items there were no dates at all, and we tried at least to establish if a negative was from the twenties or thirties, but sometimes we couldn't even do that. And we'd try to establish the names of the people and where the photographs were taken, and the circumstances surrounding them. The whole thing took two days a week for a year.

Imogen was incredibly easy to work with. She couldn't imagine how I did it, how I could stand looking at negatives all day and writing down information, all that routine. But she didn't inter-fere with my work at all, never suggested that I do something a certain way. It was a real revelation to me to work with a person of her age. It totally changed my concept of an old person. The Maritime Museum is located in the same build-ing as the Senior Center, so I came in contact with a lot of old people, but they were often grumpy or condescending, and I never really developed any kind of relationship with any of them. Imogen was so different. She didn't con-sider herself old, and she certainly didn't con-sider herself superior because of her age. And of course she was very different from every other

Danee McFarr JUDY DATER

old person I knew because she was so active.

It was a great pleasure working in her home. The house was just amazing. It was a little studio with a very tiny kitchen, a living room, another tiny room that was really a dining room but which she kept her bed in, and a back room which was supposed to be a bedroom but was a workroom. And usually when you walked in there was no place to sit, because the chairs and the couch had things piled on them — boxes of prints and negatives, letters, swatches of cloth, books, magazines. It wasn't dirty; she just had so much stuff that she had to pile it on chairs. There was a work table in the back room piled high with letters and prints and so on, and the first day I went to work she said, "We're going to clear that off so you'll have a place to work." Well, we never did, and I never did have a place to work. I worked on my lap, on the couch in the living room, wherever. But it didn't really matter.

She had a routine she followed most days. The vertigo bothered her less in the mornings, and she liked to get up early — around six-thirty — and fix herself a little breakfast, watch the news on television and take time dressing. I'd get there about eight-thirty and sometimes we would work together for a while, and then she'd go off to type some letters or work in the darkroom, and then Tom Eckstrom would come around eleven. She always made lunch, she'd insist on it; usually a big salad, a really healthy lunch, and we'd sit out on the back porch and eat and talk. Really nice. During lunch, or right before it, we'd go over the mail. That was always a treat, because she got a pile of mail, fan letters, print orders, always something interesting. Imogen would read through it while she was eating. "Listen to this," she'd say, and read something funny or outrageous. In the afternoon she'd begin to slow down, but by then the visitors would come anyway. Sometimes she would go out to the bank or drop off the laundry, or tramp down the hill for her little bag of groceries and maybe a beer for Tom. Tom or I would always offer to do these things, but she always refused. Then about four-thirty she took what she called her flop. She'd lie on the bed and sometimes she'd doze off, but she always denied it. I'd apologize for waking her and she'd say, "I wasn't sleeping, I just had my eyes closed." "Imogen, you were snoring." I usually left when she took her flop and often there were visitors coming later to take her to dinner or some opening. She was a lot less tired than I was at the end of the day, and she went out a lot more than I did. She did cut down a little bit toward the end, but she was still incredibly active, socially as well as in business.

And the visitors kept coming. Strangers would drop by, especially in the summer, and she'd invite them in and they'd stay for two or three hours. Afterward she'd complain, but she wouldn't let me turn them away. She'd talk endlessly on all kinds of subjects, not just photography, and she was always interested in what they were doing. Usually she tried to discourage them from going into photography — she'd tell them to become gardeners or something — but she was really interested in their lives. So there was a conflict. She wanted to work but she thought it was important to spend time with the visitors too.

She wasn't photographing much during the time I worked for her, partly because of the vertigo, partly because she was very busy with other things, trying to wrap up years of back correspondence. I did go along with her once when she photographed a woman named Bobbie Libarry for *After Ninety*. I had heard of her through a tattoo artist, Lyle Tuttle. Bobbie had been completely tattooed in 1915 for a life with the carnival. She was then eighty-three, not over ninety, but when I told Imogen about her, she was enthusiastic. Bobbie was in the hospital then. She had been in an accident and was partly paralyzed, and was in and out of the hospital. So we went there to photograph her, and Bobbie immediately took a liking to Imogen. They talked a lot, and then Imogen got her out of bed and into a chair and started to photograph. Imogen usually kept on talking to people while she was photographing, but I was thinking of doing an article about the tattooed lady, as we called her affectionately, so I was asking Bobbie questions and was taping the whole thing. Imogen took two or three shots and then casually said, "Oh, will you take your gown off?" Bobbie hesitated a moment, but then she dropped it a little bit and Imogen said, "A little more," and then she dropped it so that she was nude from the waist up.

I asked Bobbie about that later, and she said she never would have taken her clothes off for anyone else—even in her younger days in the carnival she always wore at least a bathing suit—but she was very comfortable with Imogen.

It was difficult working in the hospital room, though, and the session didn't result in many good shots, so later we went to Bobbie's house to photograph her, and that was much better. The portrait used in the book is beautiful. Here is this eighty-three-year-old woman, not a beautiful woman, but looking very beautiful, very calm and contented. Her hands are folded and her breasts come right down to her hands, and it's all tattoos, solid tattoos. At first glance you can't really tell it's a naked woman; the tattoos look almost like lace. Most people who look at it do a double take, and when they realize she is tattooed, most are really repelled. Not by the photograph, because it's a beautiful photograph, but by the fact this woman has done this to herself. So the photograph always gets strong reactions, and Imogen was very proud of it—thought it was one of the best portraits she'd done. And people agree, but there's always that negative attitude about tattoos.

I mentioned the session to Lyle Tuttle, the man who had told me about Bobbie, and he said he'd certainly like Imogen to photograph him. I said she was only photographing old people now, but when I mentioned it casually to her one day— "Gee, I know this man who is tattooed all over"— she immediately forgot that she wasn't photographing people under ninety anymore. So we arranged a session and she photographed him. He also didn't like posing in the nude, but Imogen casually told him to take his clothes off, so what could he do?

After about a year, my work was all done and it was time for Imogen to concentrate on photographing for *After Ninety* and to get the Trust really going. So I was to continue working for her as administrator of the Trust, running the business part of it. We had to transfer all the negatives from the house into my new office, and it was really a rather traumatic time. It was traumatic for me because I had to leave that really pleasant environment to work in an office by myself, and traumatic for Imogen because she had to give up seventy-five years of negatives she had been living with. She said she was glad, and she could finally get that back room cleaned out, but I knew she was really sad to have them leaving her house.

TOM ECKSTROM, *part 1*

Tom Eckstrom, photographer, Imogen's last assistant

I began working for Imogen in January 1975. It was supposed to be for a day or two, but I was there for a year and a half. For the first three or four months I just spotted prints, things like that, and then one day she asked to see some of my own prints. She looked them over—didn't say anything, but then she gave me some undeveloped film and her formula, and told me to develop it. So I started developing her film, and then about a week or two later I started printing for her. "After seventy-five years in the darkroom," she said, "I've had enough!"

Not long after that she started work on *After Ninety*. The book was her main concern, but she also began to spend a lot of time distributing her possessions. She said she wasn't going to be around forever—not in an unhappy way, though—and she was thinking about who was going to get the platinum prints, and so on. And she was working on the Trust. I think Imogen thought it was off to a good start, but she wanted to be an influence on it while she could. She couldn't believe the money it was generating! I guess she'd lived all her life—in most respects a very happy life—

with a limited amount of money, and she just couldn't relate to suddenly having money. She felt that it was the Trust's money, not hers. The money in the little bank account on Green Street was hers, and all that big stuff down on Folsom Street was somebody else's money. We really had to twist her arm to get her to spend any of it. Every once in a while her checking account would run pretty low, or a tax bill was due, and

I'd call Danee McFarr or Arthur Shartsis, and one of them would call back to tell her a check was coming from the Trust as part of her share. "Oh, no," Imogen would say, "I can't take that —that's Trust money. No, no, I'm all right." So I'd show up with a thousand-dollar check and have to make up some cockamamy story. "Imogen, this is the Trust's money, but it's some kind of accounting runover and they have no place to

On the Johnny Carson show, 1976 LEO HOLUB

put it, so we have to keep it in your checking account for a little while." And after a couple of weeks she'd forget about it.

One morning Imogen answered the phone, and when she put it down she said, "Can you imagine, they want me to be on the Johnny Carson show!" Apparently their talent scout had seen the *Esquire* article on the ten top photographers with Judy Dater's picture of Imogen. Then they looked up the books on her and talked to Don Ellegood at the University of Washington Press, who put them in touch with Imogen. So for about a week and a half Imogen was really debating about it. "Should I do it, or shouldn't I? What do you think?" Well, at first I thought it really wasn't her style. But then someone—I think it was Arthur Shartsis—told her, "Listen, if you go on that show it will be great promotion for the book and the Trust." That made sense to me, and I started urging her too, and she finally decided to do it.

So in April 1976 we went down to Los Angeles, where she stayed with friends for three or four days. On the night of the show I picked her up at their place. She was sitting there waiting, alone, all dolled up in a purple and orange dress. I think she was nervous but she wouldn't let on. After we got to the studio, they took her to a little dressing room with a card on the door saying "Imogen Cunningham." They gave her some business papers to sign, and then someone brought in a stack of her books to autograph and Imogen became a little easier. At first she refused any makeup, but finally she said, "My nose *does* get a little red," and she let the makeup artist powder her nose—but that was it. Then we went to the green room, where all the guests sit and watch the monitors, waiting their turn.

Imogen was the last one to go on. It was a typical Johnny Carson show, and she sat there,

her hand on her cane, stoney faced. Carson would make one of his silly cracks, and she'd turn to me and say in a really loud voice, "What are they laughing at? That's not funny." And I'm trying to get her to lower her voice. Then partway along, the producer came in and asked her what she thought of the show. "Bunch of crap," she snapped. "The most ridiculous thing I've ever seen." And I'm thinking, "Oh no, what's she going to do on the show!" Finally the third guest started winding down. Nobody had told us anything, but I took Imogen by the arm and walked her over behind the curtains, and told her they were all sitting out there on the right-hand side. Then Carson said, "IMOGEN CUNNINGHAM!" and I gave her a little nudge out between the curtains and ran back to the green room to watch.

Well, it had been a pretty ho-hum night until then, but suddenly everyone in the green room was glued to the monitor, and everyone started going nuts! I mean everyone—the technicians, the sound guys, and the cameramen backstage were all screaming with laughter. The producer was running around saying, "Why haven't we had her on before? We must have her back!" Everyone was just going crazy. And they fell in love with her. After the show everyone usually leaves right away, but the guests all stayed around, Carson leaning over his desk. And Robert Blake—Baretta—said, "Can I give you a kiss?" "No," said Imogen, "I don't want any of your germs." But he bent over and gave her a quick peck on the cheek anyway, and she picked up her cane and screeched, "You wretch!" as he went running out. Then a lot of the audience came down to the stage to talk with her too. When we finally left she was as cool as if she had just gone to the drugstore. "Well, how do you think I did?" she said. She knew exactly how she had done. It was quite an evening.

ADRIAN AND JOYCE WILSON

Adrian Wilson, book designer, printer, and author, and Joyce Lancaster Wilson, actress, author, and illustrator

Adrian: During the fifties, when I had a combined commercial printing and book design business, the University of California Press asked me to design a book on the painter Morris Graves. I had known him during the war when I was at a conscientious objectors' camp in Oregon. Morris had finally been released from the Army as a hopeless case, and he came down to the camp to find some congenial spirits. I had seen a beautiful photograph of Morris by Imogen Cunningham in a museum exhibition, and I was particularly eager to have it for the book, so I called her up. She said she'd love to have me use it, and insisted on bringing it right down so she could see my shop. She came and snooped all around. It turned out that her brother was a printer, and he had what she said was the cleanest shop she'd ever seen. I doubt if mine competed, but evidently she liked the atmosphere.

Over the next few years I used to see her at parties occasionally, that's all. But then in the fall of 1963 she heard that I was going to have surgery, and she called up.

Joyce: I answered the phone and Imogen was very direct: "I hear Adrian's going into the hospital for open-heart surgery. I want to come over and take a lot of pictures of him in case he doesn't pull through. When can I come?" She didn't actually say, "because I think he's going to die," but she was pretty blunt.

So she came over one afternoon to a very tense house. She was carrying all her own equipment and lights, and she set herself up in the studio where the press is.

Adrian: The idea was that I should kneel below the press, practically underneath it, and my head would be contrasted to all its wheels and gears. There I was in a desperate situation, trying to finish all my work, totally uncomfortable in that position, and here was this madwoman carrying on about how she had to get a picture of me before I was gone.

About two weeks later, after I had come

through the operation, Imogen brought the pictures to the hospital. I looked miserable and under strain in them, and she said she was totally dissatisfied too, and just dumped them all into the wastebasket. The Trust may still have the negatives, though.

Ten years went by before I worked with Imogen—on her second book, *Imogen!*, during 1973. In 1970, the year the first book [*Imogen Cunningham: Photographs*] appeared, she had received a Guggenheim Fellowship to allow her to review all her files, to print negatives that had never been printed before, and generally to take a fresh look at her work. As a result she discovered a lot of first-rate images that had been forgotten, or that had never even been printed, and these plus some of her most recent photographs were to be the basis of a new book. That Guggenheim, incidentally, meant a great deal to Imogen, not just for the practical help, but as a sign of recognition. On her eighty-seventh birthday, just after she'd gotten the news, Herb Caen reported the award in his column in the *San Francisco Chronicle*, describing Imogen as eighty-four. She immediately got on the phone to tell him that she was *not* eighty-four, but eighty-seven!

When she began to plan the new book she called me to ask if I would be interested in designing it. Then I got an official letter from the publisher, the University of Washington Press, so we made a date to go over the photographs at her place. The Press also sent down a box of thirty or forty photographs for me to look over, and they seemed right up to the standards of the first book. The day of the appointment I took the box and some books I wanted to show Imogen to the car, in a kind of rush because I was late for the appointment. Somehow, by the time I got to Imogen's the box had absolutely vanished! I must have set it on the roof of the car as I was putting the other things in and just slammed the door and drove away. I retraced my route— with Imogen and Margery Mann waiting for an hour and a half—stopping at every block and looking under every car between my place and

Adrian and Joyce Wilson JUDY DATER

Imogen's. But I didn't find the photographs. I reported the loss to the police, and finally I went back to Imogen's, thinking, "What a terrible way to begin a book!" Imogen took it very calmly, saying she had duplicates of most of the prints and negatives of the rest. She just brought out some more photographs, and pretty soon the three of us were choosing prints and finding duplicates or substitutes, and the whole design process was started.

The lost photographs never did turn up. One day, going along the same route, I saw the remnants of the box, but it was empty. Someone somewhere has forty very valuable Imogen Cunningham prints and probably doesn't even know what they are—but at least they're unsigned.

Joyce: The book was just about finished as Imogen's ninety-first birthday was approaching, so we called the binder on the morning of her birthday and arranged to have the first copy ready to present that day. We brought it over to her, and in between the constant phone calls she was getting I managed to ask her what she was going to do to celebrate her birthday. "Oh, Joyce," she said, "you don't celebrate an odd number like ninety-one!"

Adrian: I was working on the big Ansel Adams book, *Images 1923–1974,* at the same time, and when it came out I showed Imogen a copy. She just shook her head. "I can't stand books that are so large! I like a book you can take to bed with you." "But Imogen," I said, "two people could take that book to bed with them and read it together." "People don't go to bed together to read a book," she said.

Adrian Wilson, 1963
IMOGEN CUNNINGHAM

Joyce: She picked away at Ansel regularly, yet she respected him very much, and he did her. It was strange. Of course he was young enough to be her son, believe it or not! They're twenty years apart, and perhaps that had something to do with it. Or perhaps it was because their focus on subject matter was so entirely different.

Adrian: And of course Ansel was so successful, and apparently wealthy, and Imogen always made a point of his success and that she was Mrs. Forgotten—until she got her Guggenheim when she was eighty-seven. That put her on the map. And Ansel probably recommended her for the fellowship.

Imogen was totally undemanding to work with, perfectly content to let me say what images would go with what in the book, and whether the reproduction tonality was right. As for her attitude toward her own photography, I must say she wasn't fussy about really superior print quality, or cropping and composition. The important thing was the image as it happened the moment she took it. She had a way of focusing on a person's expression and surrounding the face with an atmosphere that didn't take over. She would often let hands, or other parts of the anatomy, run off the photograph—which drove me crazy, because in reproducing it we had to lose an eighth of an inch more all around. When her son Ron prints her work he tends to intensify the background and get more detail. He always says, "My mother was the world's worst print-maker. She couldn't make a print to save herself." I doubt that!

She did have some set ideas about presenting the work with a certain aesthetic simplicity. She'd say, "I like only black and white," and that was that. She seemed to like a lot of space around her pictures—she didn't want a book with bleeds or dynamic layouts. And she was for traditional proportions. But of course she wasn't against experimental things—her own numerous double exposures show that—but for a book I think she felt everything should be done as simply and directly as possible.

I saw a lot more of Imogen after she started the Trust and asked me to be one of its trustees. Checks had to be signed, and there were the meetings, of course. At one meeting at Arthur Shartsis's office we were debating what we should charge for her prints. Someone suggested one hundred fifty dollars would be about right, but Imogen said she would like to get two fifty. We thought that seemed a little high, so Imogen asked the price of Dorothea Lange's prints. One hundred fifty dollars. "Well," said Imogen, "there are two differences between me and Dorothea. One, I'm avaricious, and two, she's dead. So two hundred fifty."

Joyce: Imogen had quite a sizable estate when she died, but I doubt if any amount of money would have changed her lifestyle. Toward the end, when she had a bit more money, she was just as frugal about herself and her living quarters and daily habits as she'd ever been.

Adrian: She had a tremendous sense of responsibility for her finances and for the welfare of her children. And she had the forethought to set up the Trust, get all her business settled and arrange for people to carry on.

Joyce: But she waited until she was ninety to do it. Evidently at the age of ninety it occurred to her for the first time that she wasn't going to live forever.

Imogen was an extraordinary combination of unpretentiousness and self-confidence. There was no preciousness about her work or her lifestyle. It was all very direct. She made you feel that when you are really mature you make your own choices, absolutely. You don't have to worry about what other people like or what's in style—you please yourself. I think that was true for most of Imogen's life. She did what she wanted, she wore what she liked, she pleased herself. That often happens with people who live alone for many years, and it was significant that she didn't want to share her house with anyone, even toward the end when she was ill from time to time. She wanted to retain her simple household, because she had chosen everything the way she wanted it, and it was a very creative world for her.

She was very content. She may not have been forty years before, but she certainly was when we knew her.

Tom Eckstrom JUDY DATER

118

CHAPTER VIII

After Ninety

TOM ECKSTROM, *part 2*

Imogen formulated the idea for *After Ninety* in April 1975, not long after I had begun to work for her, and she started right in on it. She told me: "We're going to do a book. It's going to be called *After Ninety*, and it's going to be about old people, but you know, old people who still have their wits, who are still doing things." In other words, people like herself. The first time she mentioned it, it was as if she had been working on it for a couple of years, organizing and planning. She already had a list of names in a little book, and she started phoning. "Hello, I'm Imogen Cunningham. Do you know who I am?" Sometimes they'd say yes, sometimes no. And she'd say, "Well, anyway, I'm doing a book on old age, and I want you in it." Of course I couldn't hear the other end of the conversation, but often there'd be some murmuring, and then she'd say, "I'm ninety-two years old and I'm coming to you, so don't worry about that!" It was very funny. "The decrepit ones," she used to call old people, including herself as well.

She used mostly her 2¼ when we went out and the 4 x 5 at home. I set it up for her because her vertigo bothered her off and on, and she couldn't get under the cloth long enough to focus without getting dizzy.

Almost all the photographs for the book were done in the morning. We'd set up an appointment at someone's house for ten o'clock, and at ten sharp we'd hit. She'd charge right in and start working. That was the beauty of her technique. She was simple, direct—"charismatic" is overused, but it was something like that. A lot of the people were nervous, but she had that sparkle in her eye, that evil little smile, and those wisecracks. It was like giving them a shot before they knew it was going to hurt. She really charmed them.

She'd be chatting and at the same time saying, "Tom, pull down that shade . . . open this one more . . . more light over here . . . haul those curtains out of the way. . . ." She was a little dynamo, completely took over, but she did it in a very nice way. We got to be a real team. I knew the way she operated, and I think that's why we worked together so well. I had to be very quick, ready whenever she held out her hand for a holder of film, or whatever, and she'd go right on talking to the person—not about what she was doing, but about something the sitter was interested in. If we were photographing a doctor or an architect, she'd have fifteen stories on that profession. She could always produce some little pearl to keep them at ease. Before you knew it we had a roll of film or a dozen 4 x 5 negatives. The average sitting took only twenty minutes at her place, maybe half an hour if we went to someone's house.

Her subjects never knew what hit them, but they enjoyed the experience. Some of them were fairly prominent, but some weren't, and they were flattered to be chosen for the book. And meeting Imogen was an experience in itself.

I think Imogen did the book knowing it was going to be her last effort, though she never alluded to that. She never felt that she had absolutely finished it. There was an Indian medicine man, or woman, up in Ukiah she wanted to do, and a couple of other people.

When I first started representing Imogen, her second book, *Imogen!*, had been out about a year, and I immediately started talking to her about doing a third, as the first two had been very successful. Other people had been suggesting the same thing, so she started looking through her archives again. This went on for about six months, but then she said, "This is boring. I took all these pictures a long time ago. Why don't I go out and do some new work?" This was probably early in 1975. She had stopped taking portraits. As late as 1974 you could go to Imogen Cunningham and have your portrait taken for one hundred dollars, but now, at age ninety-two, she was becoming more selective and wanted to do other things. She used the line, "I only take pictures of people older than me." That line began to stick, and I think it was the germ of the idea for *After Ninety*. She worked out the idea with Don Ellegood of the University of Washington Press, and began taking pictures. Age alone wasn't enough to qualify. She wanted interesting people, so when she ran into trouble finding the right types, she expanded the concept and took people in their late eighties, younger than herself. The really significant thing is that somebody of ninety-two would say, "I'm starting a new project."

When Imogen visited the old people to photograph them, she had the sense that they were old, but she wasn't. She was so much more energetic than they were, a celebrity, and so she came to service them in a funny way. She'd stop and chat, and be sure they were okay. There were four or five people she photographed whom she went back to see later and did things for.

She loved telling the story of the farmer she photographed. He liked the photograph and ordered a dozen large prints and four wallet size, or something like that. Anyway, a dozen photographs would have been much too expensive for most people. Imogen, of course, made them for him, and when she delivered them he gave her some vegetables in exchange. Then he realized that that probably wasn't enough, so he went out and picked a big tray of wild raspberries for her. She clearly thought this was more than enough compensation. She realized that in the relative scale of values, his spending all that time picking wild raspberries for her was equal to what she had done. She got such a kick out of it, and it was important to her that he had given her something of himself—better than handing her a thousand-dollar bill.

There was one group of people she photographed for *After Ninety* who had not done anything particularly unique. They were simply old, a group of nuns. She went to a rest home and the attendants just wheeled out half a dozen nuns: *Present for photograph*! She was deeply shocked. It was so wrong, the way these people were presented—as if they had been wound up to have their pictures taken. She couldn't do it. She had to start over again, creating the mood she wanted, individualizing them as human beings.

She was always sensitive to this need for individual dignity, perhaps more so than the subjects themselves. In fact I think there is a change in the photographs in *After Ninety*. Before that, with some exceptions, her photographs of people tended to be straight on; this time the people are idealized to some extent. The picture of the tattooed lady, for instance. She took a series of pictures of her, and she clearly picked the most dignified one. I believe the woman had trouble with her left eye, and the left eye of the picture is in shadow—and it's not characteristic for Imogen to use harsh shadows. The way the woman was posed, with her hands folded across her breasts, maximizes the dignity of an individual that age.

Imogen told me a number of times that she tried never to photograph anyone the first time they met. She tried to meet her sitters, find out about them, who they were, and then go back and take the pictures. This was a problem with the old people. It was a labor just to see them once, and then she had to shoot the photograph at the same time.

I've always had the sense that she had done absolutely the best she could by these people. Maybe she felt that she too was getting old, and it was a look at herself. The shock of seeing those old people contributed to her not going to a rest home.

The book just ended—there was no date at which it was finished. She was pretty well done at the beginning of 1976, the contract with the University of Washington Press was on my desk, and at that point she realized that she was pretty well done with everything and was ready to die.

She started looking at rest homes. It was a very bad experience for her—she couldn't stand it. We discussed the possibility of a live-in maid, not because she was becoming incompetent, but because she didn't have the same energy, and she should have someone there with her in case something happened. She clearly began to get older fast, and she sensed it. I remember her calling me and asking if the book could come out sooner, but Ellegood said it was impossible, the publication was still a year off. So she realized she was probably not going to live to see the book. But the book was done, the Trust was running, her estate was in order, and everything was in good hands. She was done with life, and that was that. She died. And I think all that was tied together.

Imogen reveled in being a celebrity. I think she'd like this book. She felt anybody could say whatever they liked about her after she died, and that would be the most legitimate criticism of all. She'd probably think this book was a terrific idea, but if she didn't, she wouldn't oppose it. She'd say, "Have you seen this interview?" "I never realized that." "I like that picture . . . boy, that one of Shartsis is terrible!" But I think she'd like it. She liked people who did things in depth, and she had no sense of editorial control. If you said it, that was fine; she could live with it.

JACK WELPOTT

Jack Welpott, photographer, professor at San Francisco State University

The first time I met Imogen was at that commemorative workshop for Edward Weston at Esalen. One of the high points was to be a panel with Imogen and Ansel Adams. I was to be the moderator, sitting in an easy chair, and they would sit next to me on a kind of love seat, which I thought was pretty funny. As I recall, Ansel was late, and Imogen sat on the little settee waiting for his entrance, already upstaged. In any event, Ansel arrived and immediately took center stage, talking very eloquently about Weston, with all the students listening attentively. Then they came forward and got down on their knees in front of him and started taking pictures of him. Some were taking Imogen too, but mostly Ansel. Suddenly Imogen got up and left. That left me in a peculiar position, since now I had nothing to moderate. Well, I thought, she's an old lady, she's probably just gone to the john.

Or maybe she's mad about what's happening here and just walked out. But in a couple of minutes she came bustling back in with a Rollei around her neck, and immediately she knelt down in front of this row of students who were taking pictures of Ansel and she moved right down the line, taking a picture of each one of them. Of course she completely upstaged Ansel— that was the end of his discourse. The whole thing broke up into a hilarious exchange between her and Ansel and the students.

That was my first encounter with Imogen. Of course I knew a lot about her, but I never had had the guts to go knocking at her door. The students used to come in with all sorts of anecdotes about her. I remember one of them telling me about being at an exhibition and looking at a very sexy photograph of a beautiful girl, when a little old lady came up to him and stuck her elbow into his ribs and said, "You like that a lot, young man?" Imogen Cunningham, of course. The students were always telling me about conversations they had had with her, so I not only knew her work, I was very conscious of her presence in San Francisco.

At first I was intimidated by her quick tongue, but as I came to know her in situations that were increasingly more friendly, I became less reserved. And since I'd met her in the context of a homage to Edward Weston, sometimes I would talk with her about him. In one very relaxed moment we were joking about Weston's many loves, and I said to her, "Tell me, Imogen, did you have an affair with Weston?" "My land, no," she said, "that little runt?"

She liked to put a pin in people's balloons when it seemed appropriate. She did it to me on a number of occasions when I was expounding opinions that were not well thought out. One night I was ranting about commercial photographers—the New York photographers who were suddenly moving into the world of art photography because their financial underpinnings were slipping, their high fashion and magazine work was drying up. "Then you don't think much of me either," Imogen said. "I'm a commercial photographer. I take photographs for a living, you know." Immediately she put the whole thing into a different perspective for me, and I had to redefine my thinking.

I always wondered what she thought of my photographs, but I never had the courage to ask. When I had that big retrospective at the San

Jack Welpott JUDY DATER

Francisco Museum I watched her looking at the photographs. She looked very carefully, and in fact she stopped in front of one for a long time and had a very lengthy conversation about it with a friend, a rather elderly, conservative-looking person. They kept pointing to the photograph. It was a little on the risqué side, in fact maybe blatantly sexual, and I fantasized that Imogen was explaining that it was all right for me to do that. I never had the guts to ask her for a critique. I felt that would be putting her on the spot, and she didn't like to do that sort of thing.

In the last few years of her life I was always photographing Imogen on a casual level. For some reason we never had a serious session, perhaps because I was a little intimidated about even trying it. But I made a lot of casual photographs of her, and at one point I became conscious that when I got the camera out she would always put herself in a situation and use her body in a way that would make my kind of photograph. She knew I was interested in hand gesture, and she immediately fell into doing things with hands. She knew I liked a certain kind of environmental situation, and she'd move herself into something like that. I took that as a high compliment, because it demonstrated that she was quite aware of the kind of photographs I was making.

My own work was influenced by Imogen's, primarily in portraiture. Very few portraitists in recent years have been masters of available light —indoors, that is. Imogen had an incredible ability to make really strong portraits by window light, so I look at her work a lot to see how she

Imogen Cunningham, 1975 JACK WELPOTT

used natural light to expose images to get a strong portrait. And I look at her portraits to see how she structured her images, to study the kind of integrity with which the background and the subject operate. I used to listen with some fascination to her talking about looking for a location for a particular portrait. The one of the poet Roethke—she kept talking about seeing this alley and realizing it was the perfect place to photograph him, though it took her a long while to get him there. That kind of foresight, that awareness of how to put people in the setting that would make a powerful image, fascinated me.

Often people feel that the so-called fine-art photographer doesn't have a major impact on the social scene. By fine-art photographer I mean someone like Imogen, who is interested in self-expression, as opposed to a photodocumentarian like Dorothea Lange, who is making a social point. But in fact I think Imogen is a prime example of how someone who is simply working on a highly expressive level can have an impact on the culture. Imogen was a step along the way in the liberation of the woman to function as an equal in photography. She was one of several women who proved that women can be as good in the visual arts as men, can be as innovative, can be as influential in the whole mainstream of art. Her photographs of the male nude on Mount Rainier in 1915 are a clear example of that, and they also tie into the liberation of women generally. There was a woman doing something that at that time was totally improper for a woman. Whether or not they were great photographs, whether or not the model was her husband, those photographs were a declaration that women had the same right as men. If men can observe women nude, as they have been doing forever in the history of art; if they can express their sensual, sexual side by painting or photographing women nude, then women have the same right to observe the male nude. As far as I know Imogen was the first woman to do that. So those photographs were a historical statement of women's rights—but she was not thinking of that. She was just a fearlessly independent woman who took what was her right.

She proved, too, that women can be "masters" in the visual arts in the sense that certain people are identified as masters in the history of art. I can't think of any woman in the visual arts before Julia Margaret Cameron who could be called a master, and she probably couldn't have done it in painting. I'm sure her painter friends like Watts thought she was just a quaint lady dabbling in this silly photography. But she was a master, and the next one was perhaps Gertrude Käsebier, and then Imogen. So Imogen was a pioneer, extremely important, as good as the men around her—namely, Adams and Weston—as good as Dorothea Lange. A really pivotal person in the history of photography.

There was a special heroism to that role, and it probably caused her a great deal of heartache. It's easy to look back and see the rejection of her nudes in a humorous light, but imagine how devastating it may have been for her to hear all that criticism. And then there was the business of trying to be a serious photographer when pressures of family and society suggested that she should be a wife and mother. It took a lot of courage to stay with it and not to become just a little housewife. Dorothea Lange was a hero too, but perhaps it was a little easier for her. She chose to deal with the problems of society, a role that certainly had more dignity surrounding it, was more acceptable than the role of the garret artist, photographing the nude, doing what she could to express herself. Imogen's role was doubly heroic.

Since Imogen didn't drive, I found myself escorting her to a lot of openings, or taking her to workshops, or to Carmel or Yosemite. She liked the attention paid her, but on the other hand she didn't want the usual courtesies—men friends kissing her, that sort of thing. "I'm not the kissy kind," she'd say. She was never demonstrative in that way. When I'd bring her home at night I always felt it essential that I should take her up to the door and maybe go inside to be sure everything was all right. But in order to carry this off there had to be a little charade between us. I would open the car door and she'd say, "This is fine, I can go from here." "Imogen," I'd say, "I come from a little community in the Middle West where a man always walks a woman to the door. I was brought up that way and you'll just have to relate to it." "All right, if you must." Then I'd walk her to the door and I'd say, "Imogen, I should come in and look around for a moment." "There's no need to do that. That's totally unnecessary." "Imogen, you'll have to allow me my chivalry, because that's the way I was brought up." So then she'd let me. We always had these funny little games. I always felt that she liked me to walk her to the door, but she needed a reason to allow it.

As time went on we became increasingly close, and she made me feel that I was wanted and needed, so long as I operated within the bounds of her not wanting to be kissed, and all the rest. The most striking thing that made me feel that we had really become close happened just before she died. I was on my way to Japan to do a workshop and stopped by to say goodbye. I walked in and the floor was littered with photographs. Danee McFarr was going through prints, and Imogen was sitting in a chair with the sunlight hitting her through the window. I remember thinking she looked sainted and very frail, but there was a real beauty about her. I could see that she wasn't feeling well, and when I asked her how she was, she said, "Well, I'm trying to die today, and I just don't seem to be able to do

it." A little while later another visitor came, and she said the same thing to him: "I'm trying to die today, and I can't seem to do it." And he responded, rather charmingly, "What's your hurry?"

We chatted for a while, but I had a powerful feeling that I wouldn't see her again. Imogen had said it was time for her to go, and if she had decided to do it, she would. So I had very strange feelings: on one level, very sad, but on another, optimistic, because she was making a choice, controlling her own fate, leaving in a dignified way. When I got up to leave I said something conventional about seeing her when I got back—and she didn't say anything. As I walked past her she reached out and grabbed my arm and held onto it and slid her hand down my arm and held my hand. It was so unlike Imogen, something she would do only in the most extreme circumstances, at least to me, and I left with the feeling that it was an intimate gesture of goodbye.

When I got to Tokyo I heard that she had died. I'll never forget that gesture. Just to show she had affection for me, she had become kissy for a moment.

Imogen Cunningham and Twinka, Yosemite, 1974 JUDY DATER

Photographs by
IMOGEN CUNNINGHAM

1 *The Dream, 1910*

2 *Veiled Woman, 1910–1912*

3 *On Mount Rainier 6, 1915*

4 *Roi Partridge, Etcher, 1915*

5 On Mount Rainier 7, 1915

6   *Family on the Beach, about 1910*

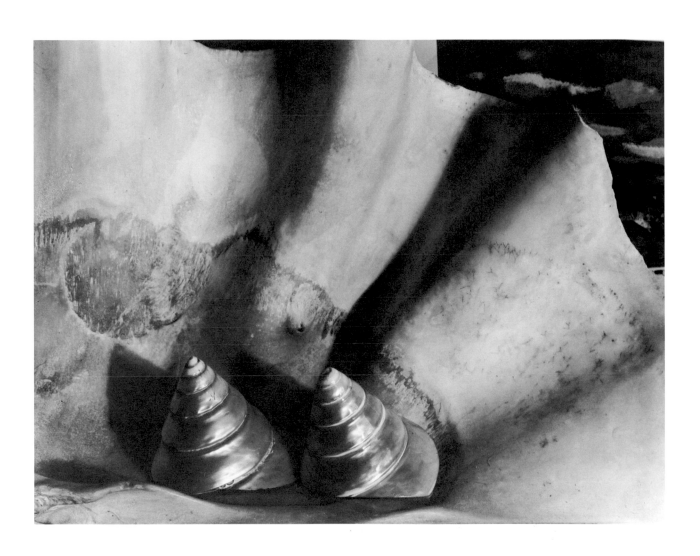

7   *Shells, about 1930*

8 *Twins with Mirror, 1923*

9 John Butler with His Mural, 1912

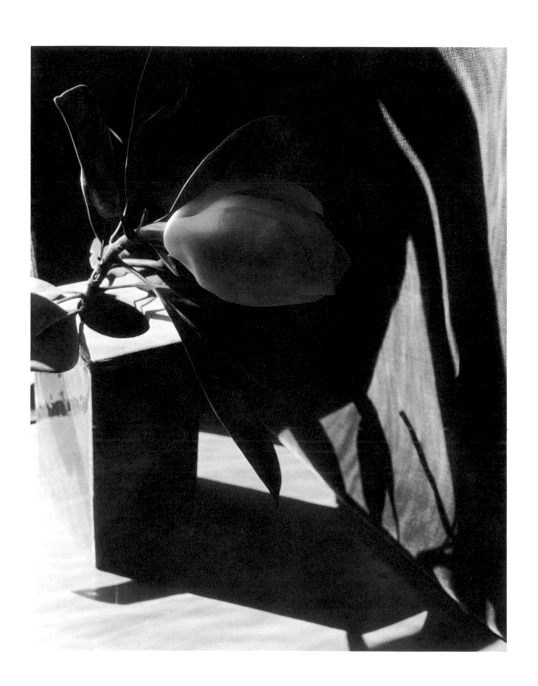

10   *Magnolia: Variations on a Theme, 1920s*

11   *Magnolia Blossom, 1925*

12 Brett Weston, 1923

13 *Edward Weston and Margrethe Mather, 1923*

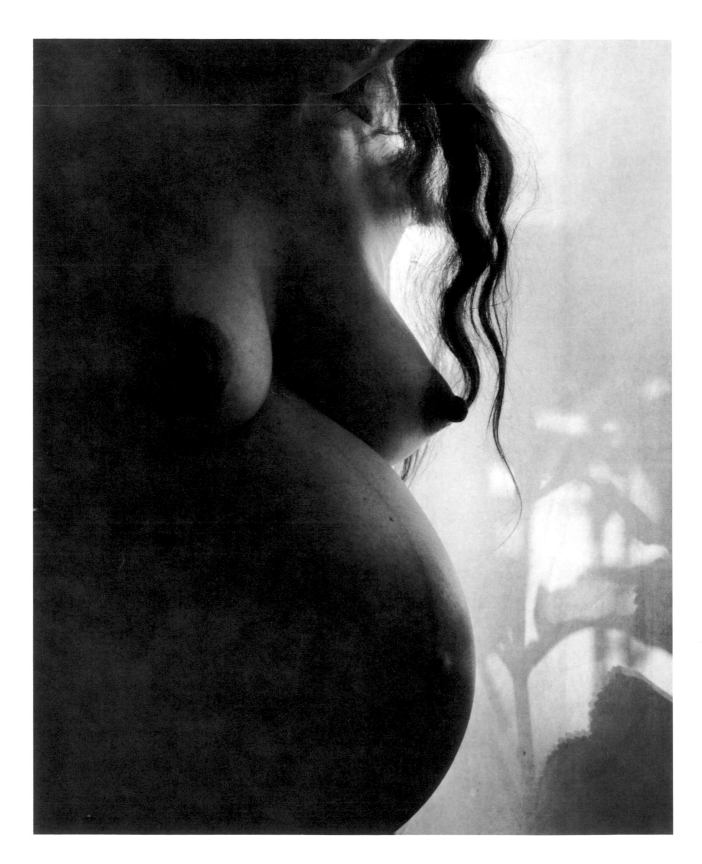

14 *Pregnant Woman, 1959*

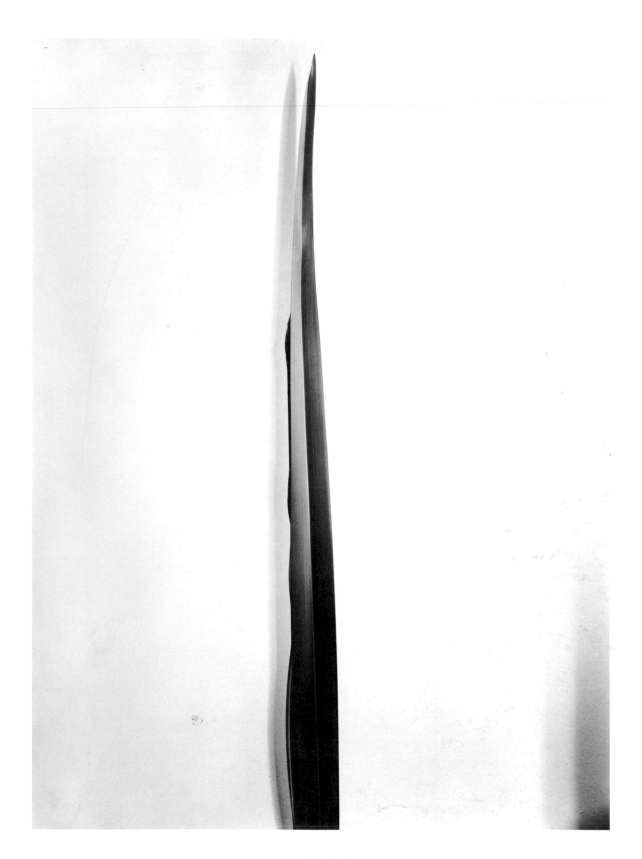

15 *Flax* (n.d.)

16   Succulent, 1920s

17   *Hands of Sculptor Robert Howard (n.d.)*

18   *Frida Kahlo Rivera, Painter and Wife of Diego Rivera, 1937*

19   *Martha Graham, Dancer, 4, 1931*

20   *Robert Irwin, Executive Director of American Foundation for the Blind, 1933*

21   *Datura* (n.d.)

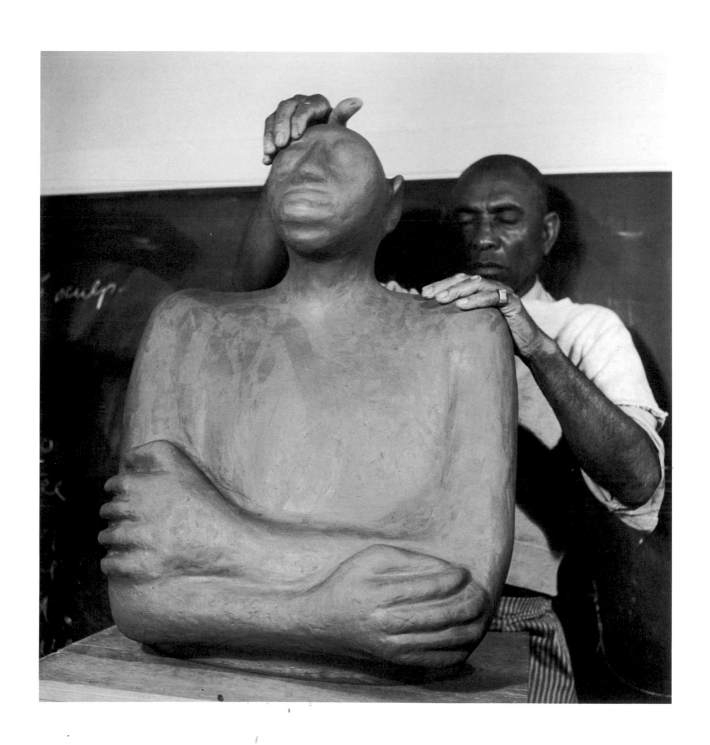

22 *Blind Sculptor, 1952*

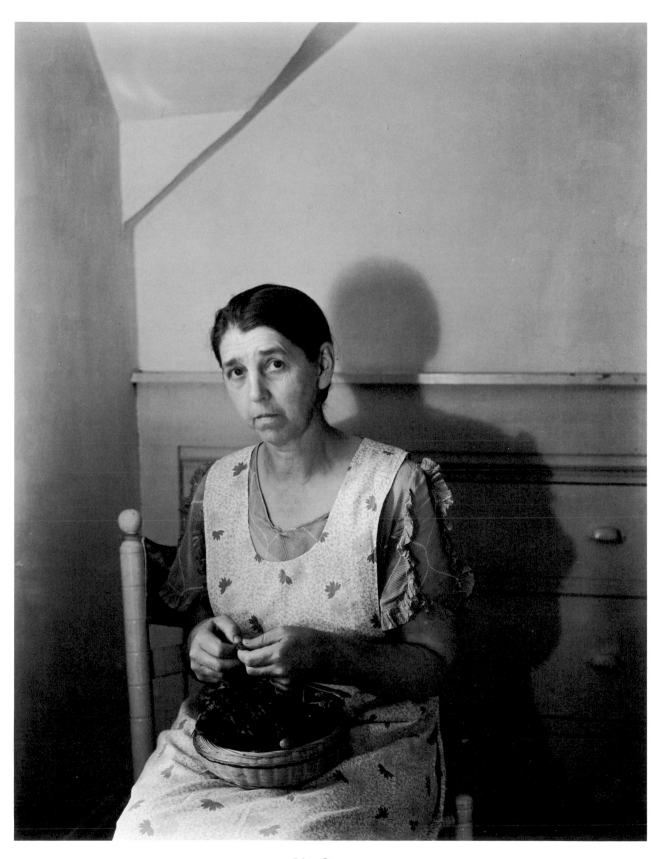

23 *Mrs. Strong, 1935*

24 *Theodore Roethke, Poet, 1959*

25 *James Stephens, Writer, 1935*

26   *Shen Yao, Professor of Linguistics at the University of Hawaii, 1938*

27 *Two Callas, about 1929*

28 *Roberta, 1959*

29 *Stapelia, 1928*

30 *José Limón, Dancer, 1939*

31 *Leaf Pattern, before 1929*

32 Nude, 1923

33 Two Sisters, 1928

34 Banana Plant, before 1929

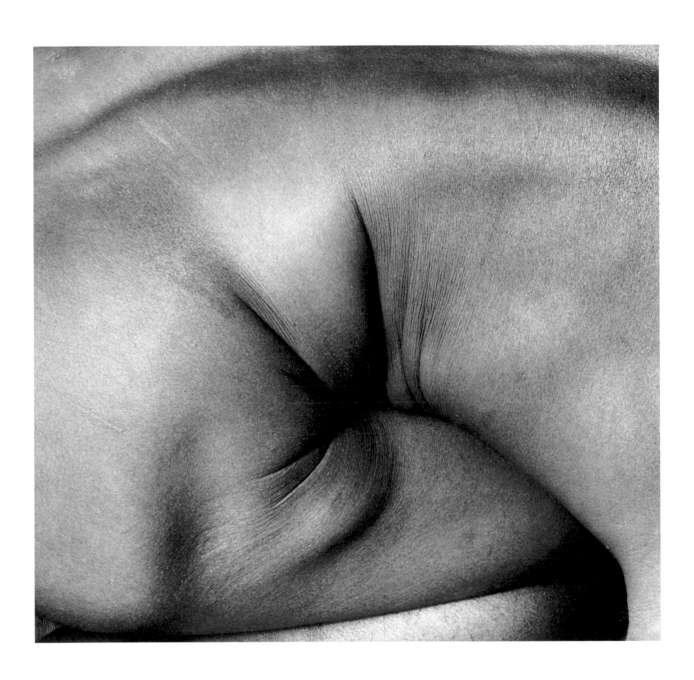

35 *Side, 1930s*

36   *Portia Hume, early 1930s*

37 *Rainwater on Oregon Beach, 1967*

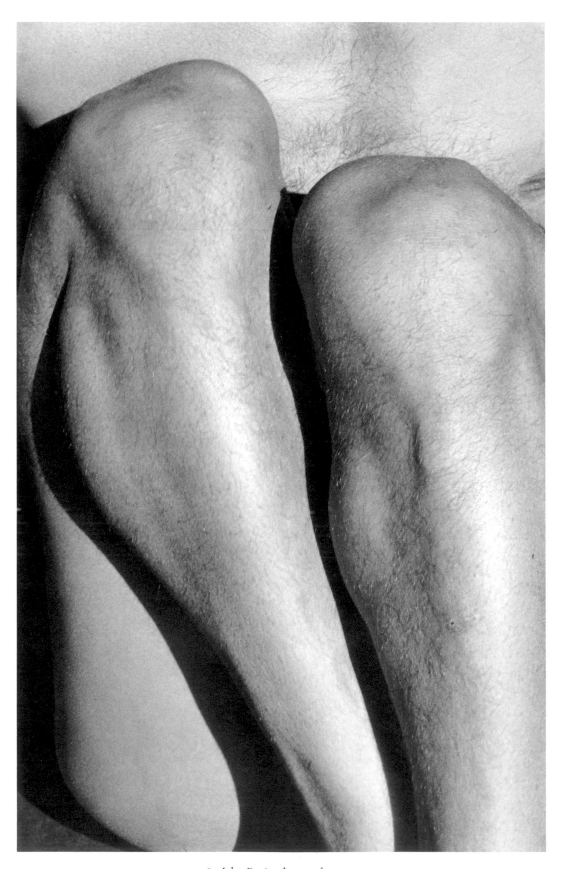

38 *John Bovingdon, early 1930s*

39   On Your Head, early 1930s

40 *Cary Grant, Actor, 1932*

41 *Magnolia Bud, 1920s*

42 *Three Vegetables, 1946*

43   Lyle Tuttle, Tattoo Artist, 1976

44 Stan, 1959

45 *Helena Mayer, Fencer, 1935*

46   *Gertrude Stein, Writer, 1937*

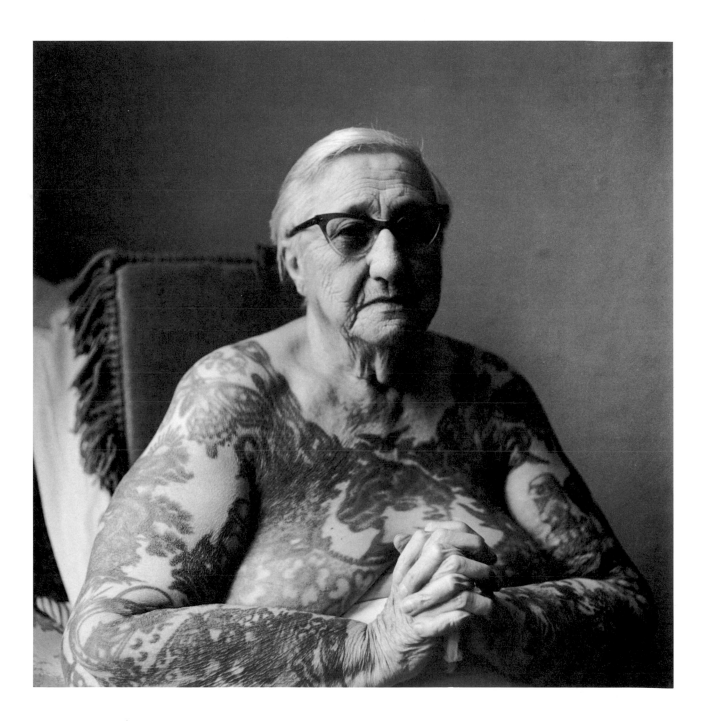

47 Irene ("Bobbie") Libarry, 1976

48   *The Poet and His Alter Ego (James Broughton, Poet and Filmmaker), 1962*

49 *Woman in Sorrow, 1964*

50 *Minor White, Photographer, 1963*

51   Alfred Stieglitz, Photographer, 1934

52   *Ansel Adams, Photographer, 1975*

53   *Wynn Bullock, Photographer, 1966*

54 *Roi with Horse's Skull, 1975*

55 *Navajo Rug, 1968*

56　Morris Graves, Painter, 1950

57   *Morris Graves in His Leek Garden, 1973*

58   My Father at Ninety, 1936

59 My Mother Peeling Apples, about 1910

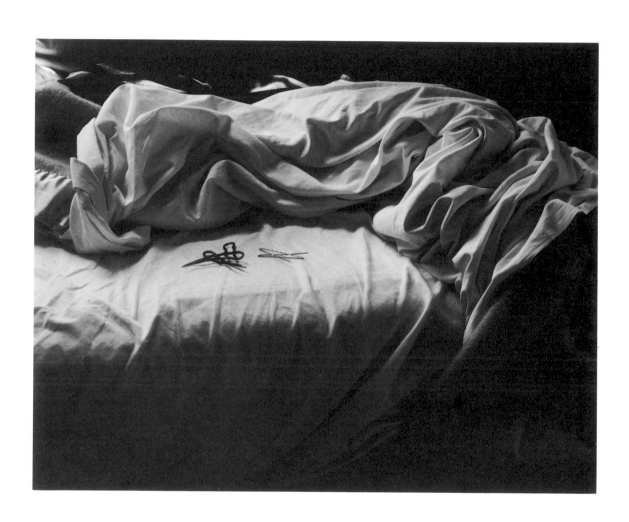

60　*The Unmade Bed, 1957*

Designed by Katy Homans

Composition in Dante by Michael & Winifred Bixler, Boston, Massachusetts

Printed in duotone by The Leether Press, Yarmouth, Maine

Paper is Karma, supplied by Northwest Paper Company

Bound by A. Horowitz and Son, Fairfield, New Jersey